OUTPERFORM THE NORM

for LEADERS

A Guide to Inspiring Peak Performance
IN AN EVER-CHANGING WORLD

SCOTT WELLE | *#1 Best Selling Author*

Copyright © 2020 by Outperform The Norm

For permission requests, speaking inquiries, and bulk order purchase options, email speaking@scottwelle.com.

All rights reserved. No part of this publication or the information in it may be quoted from or reproduced in any form by means such as printing, scanning, photocopying or otherwise without prior written permission of the copyright holder.

Terms of Use: This is a work of nonfiction. Nonetheless, the names, personal characteristics of the individuals, and details of the events have been changed to disguise identities or protect the privacy of the author's clients and students. Any resulting resemblance to persons living or dead is entirely coincidental and unintentional.

Effort has been made to ensure that the information in this book is accurate and complete, however, the author and the publisher do not warrant the accuracy of the information, text and graphics contained within the book due to the rapidly changing nature of science, research, known and unknown facts and internet.

Lastly, I don't believe in "get rich" programs - only in hard work, contributing value and serving others with excellence and consistency. As stipulated by law, I cannot guarantee your ability to get results or earn any money with the information, tools and strategies in this book. Use caution and always consult your accountant, lawyer or professional advisor before acting on this or any information related to a lifestyle change or your business or finances. You alone are the variable and are accountable for the results you get in your life, and by reading this book you agree not to attempt to hold me liable for your decisions, actions or results, at any time, under any circumstance. Sound good?

ISBN: 979-8638763978
1st edition, April 2020

Printed in the United States of America

To YOU, the leader.

BULK DISCOUNT PROGRAM FOR LEADERS

Lead or manage a team? Want them to Outperform?
Consider purchasing this book and the
supplementary resources for professional development.
Please contact scott@scottwelle.com to discuss bulk pricing options.

Leaders are Readers. Learners are Earners. Start now.

PREFACE

All is right in the world.

It's early April, 2020. The economy is booming, spring sports are in full swing and I have just returned from running the Ibiza marathon and celebrating my 40th birthday in Spain.

If only it was true. Instead, we're in the thick of a pandemic that will be remembered, forever, by everyone that's living through it.

Where were you? What were you doing? How did you handle it?

These stories will be told to children too young to realize what's happening and to those not-yet-born. Generational significance, akin to The Great Depression, WWI & WWII, 9/11 and The Great Recession of 2007.

The avalanche of tragedy that has descended upon us is unprecedented. As if the sickness, suffering and mortality weren't bad enough, financial markets have plummeted and businesses have been forced to close—for some, indefinitely.

One more thing, try stomaching all of this in isolation. Let me know how *that* tastes. Holidays without family, happy hours without friends, office meetings without...*an office*. FaceTime and Zoom were meant to be supplements, not substitutes, for human contact.

"Control the controllables" is a universal phrase in my speeches, regardless of audience. Our outcomes have, perhaps, never been more uncontrollable or uncertain; thus, making controlling our attitudes and actions never more essential.

Growing up in Minnesota, one of my favorite things to do was to play outside in a snowstorm. The harder it snowed, the happier I was. My most fun days were running full speed, with big, fluffy flakes pelting me in the face, in a blanket of white so strong that I could barely see two feet in front of me.

At times, the grim negativity of this pandemic seems like that snowstorm. It's impossibly hard to see through it. Still, one of the things that gives me hope, and has driven me to finish this book, is the daily presence and perseverance of Outperforming leaders all around us.

Leaders that, despite crisis, are committed to their best.

Leaders that show up consistently, even though their home is now their home-office.

Leaders that are being courageous. Healthcare workers, you're top of the list.

Leaders that communicate effectively by meeting people—and appreciating them—for where they are.

Leaders that continue connecting to deep, meaningful, purpose-driven work.

Leaders that cast a vision for a new normal that will look even better and brighter than our old normal.

I started this book thinking that my ideal reader would be a successful businessperson; someone climbing corporate America and taking others with them. I now believe these messages of impacting and inspiring others, transcends business. It's for the Outperformer that may lead not only in their company, but also in their family, church, community, organization or anywhere else.

I hope this book serves you, as you serve others.

LEADERSHIP BOOK BONUSES

Want even more Outperforming Resources?

My BEST personal videos and articles to motivate your team

5-part Courageous Leadership Series (audio / video) + handout

The exclusive "Alter Ego Playbook"

Shareable images from the book to inspire peak performance

FOR FREE ACCESS, PLEASE VISIT:
OutperformTheNorm.com/books

INTRODUCTION

All the hands instinctively go up.

I'm speaking to a large group of project managers and I've just asked the question:

"How many of you can think of a great leader you've had in your life?"

It's a direct question to which I've found—almost—everyone has the answer. And, after speaking to thousands of individuals, I've also found that people can answer the reverse of this question and easily think of a poor leader they've had in their life.

Leaders come in and out of our lives, in all times and types, in all shapes and sizes. They are bosses, coaches, parents, community volunteers, teachers, ministers, captains or bus drivers.

We don't choose when they show up. They just...*appear*...and inspire and impact us in profound ways, often when we least expect it.

Herein lies the first fundamental principle of leadership—there are *Appointed Leaders* and *Emergent Leaders*.

A title of "boss, teacher, captain, etc.," is only something that can be appointed by someone else. In the grand scheme of leadership, it means next-to-nothing. It may put you in the position to influence, but it's not the reason it happens. It's insufficient.

True leadership happens everyday when a person, with or without an appointed title, emerges from the pack and becomes the one others seek to follow. It can be in the boardroom, classroom or locker room. It unfolds the same way.

This leader rarely needs to speak the loudest; their voice is easily heard. They are the ones people turn to when there's conflict, pressure, change, turmoil. They may not have the biggest office, but they have the biggest impact.

Their aura breathes confidence and certainty. *We've got this.*

Leadership is like charisma: You know it when you see it but it's difficult to define—and even more difficult to describe *why* it happens and *how* to replicate it. When I watched the TV show, *Happy Days*, it wasn't easy to identify why Fonzi was so charismatic and cool. He simply...*was*.

I had a call with the head of a global speaker's bureau last week. He said, adamantly, "Scott, *by far* the most requested training topic for companies and organizations is leadership." It's popular, it's prevalent, yet the very definition of leadership still varies. Consider a few of the well-known viewpoints:

Peter Drucker: "The only definition of leadership is someone who has followers."
Bill Gates: "Leaders are those who empower others."
Warren Bennis: "Leadership is the capacity to translate vision into reality."
John Maxwell: "Leadership is influence. Nothing more, nothing less."
Dwight D. Eisenhower: "Leadership is the art of getting someone else to do something you want done because he wants to do it."
Jack Welch: "Before you are a leader, success is all about growing yourself. When you are a leader, success is all about growing others."
Henry Kissinger: "The task of the leader is to get his people from where they are now to where they have not been."[1]

None of these definitions are wrong, but in my humble opinion, they all seem incomplete; missing something. This leads to the Outperforming definition of leadership and the one which will guide the pages of this book:

> "LEADERSHIP IS A COMMITMENT TO CONSISTENTLY SHOW UP AS YOUR BEST, TO INFLUENCE AND INSPIRE OTHERS TO SEE MORE, DO MORE AND BECOME MORE, IN THE PURSUIT OF A LOFTY GOAL OR WORTHWHILE AMBITION."

INTRODUCTION

This may sound like a mouthful, but I purposely choose the definition for a few reasons:

- ✓ Leaders are committed, not interested
- ✓ Consistency builds trust from those around you: a necessity in leadership
- ✓ Unapologetically showing up as YOUR best, in front of others, is a heroic and courageous act
- ✓ We influence through communication and inspire through our actions
- ✓ We allow others "see more" by casting a vision
- ✓ We help others "do more" and "become more" by connecting to a purpose
- ✓ There is a finish line (goal or worthwhile ambition) we're moving towards; something that's bigger than ourselves

If you'd rather have a visual representation of the discrepancies between The Norm and Outperform as a leader, here it is:

THE NORM	OUTPERFORM
INTERESTED	COMMITTED
ERRATIC	CONSISTENT
TALKS AT YOU	TALKS WITH YOU
SEES CRISIS	SEES OPPORTUNITY
BE THE BEST	BE YOUR BEST
NEED LESS PROBLEMS	NEED MORE SOLUTIONS
GOOD ENOUGH	PRIDE IN EXCELLENCE
SUM OF THE PARTS	GREATER WHOLE
IT'S MY RIGHT	IT'S MY RESPONSIBILITY
INFORMATION	IMPLEMENTATION
STUCK IN PAST	STRIVE FOR FUTURE
SHRINK	SHINE
EATS FIRST	EATS LAST

INTRODUCTION

On the following pages, you'll receive my top Outperforming strategies for leaders. The first three sections are about getting the best out of YOU. The next three sections are about getting the best out of OTHERS. The tips are relatively quick and to the point, with very little fluff. They are short stories, in a scientifically proven playbook, that you can put in your leadership game plan, immediately.

Let's lead.

CONTENTS

PREFACE 4

INTRODUCTION 7

COMMIT TO YOUR BEST 15
    Attitude of Gratitude 16
    Begin with Intent 18
    The Best vs. Your Best 20
    Amplify Your Goodness 22

SHOW UP CONSISTENTLY 25
    The Crux of Consistency 26
    Winning the Mental Game of Life 27
    Manage Your Inputs 29
    The Vital 4% 31
    Remaining Resilient 35
    Daily Execution. Extraordinary Results. 39
    Be Who You Say You Are 41
    Summary Guide 44

BE COURAGEOUS 45
    Are You An Imposter? 46
    For Everybody = For Nobody 48
    Handling Hard Decisions 50
    Your Mess is Your Message 53
    The Alter Ego 55
    Crisis Considerations 59
    The One BIG Question 63
    Summary Guide 65

COMMUNICATE EFFECTIVELY 67
    A Different Pair of Shoes 68
    Be Insatiably Curious 69
    Intuitively Making Someone's Day 72
    EPP: Expectation Performance Process 73
    To Delegate is to Empower 76
    Highly Effective Teams Have THIS 79
    Working and Leading Virtually 81

    Dealing with Difficult People 85
    Put Others on the Pedestal 88
    Summary Guide 91

CONNECT TO A PURPOSE 93
    The Reason Behind It All 94
    What Do You DO? 96
    Making it a Must 98
    Manufacturing Urgency 100
    Meetings That Matter 103
    Adopt a Rallying Cry 106
    Creating a Culture of Excellence 108
    High Performance PEP Talks 112
    You're Teaching, But Not What You Think 114
    Summary Guide 116

CAST A VISION 117
    Where Are We Going? 118
    Simple Visions Sell 119
    Using Positive Future Pacing 121
    Images Speak Louder Than Words 122
    Un(certain)ty in Future Change 124
    The Special Speech Structure 126
    Summary Guide 129

CONSTRUCT YOUR GAME PLAN 131
    Tools and Projects 132
    Situational Awareness 133
    Implement with Intention 135
    Kaizen 138

ACKNOWLEDGMENTS 141

REFERENCES 143

ABOUT THE AUTHOR 146

ALSO BY SCOTT WELLE 148

SECTION 1

COMMIT TO YOUR BEST

"To give anything less than your best
is to sacrifice the gift."

ATTITUDE OF GRATITUDE

A woman slowly approaches me. She's shaking, crying.

I've just finished a speech for a group of small business owners in Cherry Creek, CO. As I see her come towards me, the emotion written all over her face, my first thought is—*Oh no! Was my speech that bad?!?!*

Normally, I let an audience member speak first, but I jump the gun: "Are you okay?" I ask.

She reassures me. "Thank you so much for talking about the power of gratitude. I recently beat stage-3 breast cancer and there were times that I was in a very dark place. One thing that kept me going was keeping a gratitude journal. It gave me strength; and gave me a reason to fight."

We smile and hug. She has no idea that my mother also had stage-3 breast cancer many years ago. I'm grateful for her, and to be able to do what I do.

Gratitude is a needle-moving Outperforming habit that enhances every area of your life. It is a lot like exercise—there are very few other things that replicate the benefits physically, mentally and emotionally. Consider the following eight advantages of gratitude:

✓ **Improved physical health**

Grateful people exercise more and take better overall care of themselves.

✓ **Develop more and better relationships**

Personally, this is never a bad thing. Professionally, if you're in business, you're in the relationship business.

✓ **Improved psychological health**

Including more happiness, fulfillment and lower risk of depression.

✓ **Increased empathy**

A MUST for getting the best out of others. Also reduced aggression.

✓ **Better sleep**

It is where the magic happens.

✓ **Improved self-esteem and confidence**

Confidence is the ONE universal trait of all Outperformers.

✓ **Reduced stress and anxiety**

I think we can all use this from time to time, right?

✓ **Increased mental strength**

Resiliency and ability to positively respond to adversity.[2]

Think about it—if you could swallow a pill and immediately see all those benefits, how much differently would you come at life?

When you are grateful, it's not that it does away with the BAD; it reinforces and anchors in the GOOD. One of the most compelling cases for gratitude is that you cannot simultaneously feel a positive and negative emotion.

Have you ever been stressed? Anxious? Angry? Overwhelmed? Defeated?

Well, you cannot experience...*THAT*...while being grateful at the same time. Try it—it won't work.

One of the easiest, most practical ways to have more gratitude in your life is to make a simple one-word shift:

I HAVE TO → I GET TO

We can all be guilty of making this mistake:

I have to go to work.
I have to get on an airplane.
I have to finish my presentation.
I have to lead this meeting.
I have to exercise.
I have to do the laundry.

Make the word shift. I promise, if you do it, you'll count more of your blessings and feel better about every single thing you do in life, personally and professionally.

BEGIN WITH INTENT

Leaders start their days with intention. They are masters of proactively planning, instead of reactively responding, to their environment.

Doing this is simple, but it's not easy. In our modern, hyper-connected age of technology where text messages, emails and social media are available to you 24/7 with the swipe of a finger, it can be very easy to get sucked into other people's agendas and to lose sight of your own.

"But, Scott, being a leader means other peoples' agendas ARE my agenda! I need to support them."

I understand your point. But what do you think sets a stronger message—being hyper-connected and reactive to people at all times, or consciously setting the example of managing your own priorities and proactively planning your day?

To start your days with intention, ask three questions:

1. **What do I need to advance to make it an Outperforming day?**

I use the word "advance" intentionally (instead of "accomplish"), because leadership almost always involves long-term projects that cannot be completed on any given day.

I come back to a football analogy:

> **INTENTION MEANS MOVING THE BALL DOWN THE FIELD AS EFFICIENTLY, AND EFFECTIVELY, AS POSSIBLE.**

Do this enough times and you'll score touchdowns, field goals, and probably, win the "game."

When you evaluate your programs, projects, procedures and tasks, what decided actions and activities will allow you to advance today? To move the ball down the field?

2. **How do I want to show up?**

When you decide how you want to show up, you become intentional about how other people see you. What do you want them to see?

Answering this question helps in two ways. First, especially if you've been with a company or organization for a long period of time, you'll maximize your interactions. Instead of thinking, "It really doesn't matter if I don't show up as my best today because I'll see them tomorrow;" you'll make each interaction count. Second, you'll have less bad days. No one answers the question, "How do I want to show up?" with "Stressed out, pessimistic, disengaged and uncaring." If you have a day going in the wrong direction, you've created a pattern interrupt. With this comes awareness and the opportunity for course correction.

3. **Who needs me to Outperform?**

Is it your customers, clients or company? Your team or direct reports? Your family, community or church?

When you anchor in who is relying on YOU to Outperform, it raises "psychological necessity" (see *Making it a Must*) and becomes non-negotiable for you to be at your best. You MUST show up. There is built-in pressure for you to perform (in a good way). Days of going through the motions are replaced with days of meaningful interactions and intentions.

THE BEST VS. YOUR BEST

The psychology of high achievement contains two different "orientations."

The first is an Ego Orientation (also called a Performance Orientation), or stacking yourself up against *someone else*, or *something else*. It's rooted in comparison. If you've ever looked out at the landscape of what you do and thought about how you can gain a competitive advantage, you're using an ego orientation.

Much of sports, business and life, is rooted in comparison. It's the desire to beat others; to be best in class. To dominate your marketplace, industry or field.

Many successful people in history have used an ego orientation, namely Michael Jordan, who had one of the most legendary Hall of Fame induction speeches of all time. Most athletes use their speech to give credit to all the people that supported and helped them get there. Not Jordan. His speech was a long list of the people who *doubted him*, all the way from the coach of his high school basketball team through his six NBA Championships. It was unique, and I give him credit for being raw and authentic.

Even though Michael Jordan was, by far, my favorite athlete of all time, watching it made me a bit sad. You can be INCREDIBLY high achieving—like Jordan—by focusing on comparison, being better than others, proving people wrong; but I wonder whether you're every truly fulfilled? It seems to be a long, lonely road.

"COMPARISON IS THE THIEF OF JOY."

Teddy Roosevelt echoed this statement and I believe it, to my core. In general, people that are higher achieving, more focused and respond better to feedback, have a Mastery Orientation, which evaluates you against you.[3] Instead of basing your standards against someone else, you're competing against your own previous performance standards.

Where are you today compared to yesterday?
Where are you this month compared to last month?
Where are you this year compared to last year?
Where are you this decade compared to last decade?

A mastery orientation is striving for better than before. That probably sounds overly simplistic, but the leaders that operate by this philosophy are not only higher achieving; they are also more motivated and fulfilled.[4]

THE best only happens when you are striving to be YOUR best.

I recently spoke for multiple offices of a national dental, vision and life insurance company. The first office, located in the Midwest, has had stable leadership, a proven track record of success, and is the frequent winner of corporate awards for "best office." They can do no wrong (or so it seems). The second office is in Mountain West. They've had turnover in staff and leadership, and even though their results have significantly improved in the last year, they're still nowhere near the level of production of the Midwest office.

When I met with this second office, instead of celebrating their growth during the last year over their own previous standards, I mostly heard negativity about how the Midwest office is still "killing it," and how, "we're never going to get where they are."

With this orientation, how motivated do you think they'll be moving forward?

I understand as a leader in charge of a team, department, division, or company, you must look outside at what other people are doing. I'm not dismissing the importance of this *at all*. What I am advocating is to carefully balance the evaluation of what OTHERS are doing with what YOU were previously doing.

I will promise you this—if you wake up every single day and focus on making your team, division, department, or company better today than it was yesterday, you'll gain the greatest competitive advantage.

AMPLIFY YOUR GOODNESS

As leaders, much of what we encounter on our teams and society is a game of tug-of-war. Pulling on one side of the rope, there's uncertainty, apathy, skepticism, fear and lack of confidence. Especially in times of change and adversity—whether in your company, community, church or Costco—you can feel the collective negative emotions. The stronger the sentiments; the stronger the pull on the rope.

> **LEADERS MUST PULL ON THE OPPOSITE SIDE OF THE ROPE WITH AN EVEN GREATER STRENGTH.**

For Outperformers, this means amplifying your goodness.

In crisis and change, if you show up the same way that you always show up, you lose the game of tug-of-war. You're overmatched by the strength of the negative. It takes a conscious and intentional effort to seize the opportunity of showing up at a greater level.

Three particular areas to focus on in amplifying your goodness:

✓ **Patience**

Change, fear and uncertainty puts people on edge. Instead of engaging their prefrontal cortex in logical, rational thought, they default to the biology of their most instinctive reactions. They seek safety and security.

We must meet this anxiety with an even greater level of patience and understanding.

✓ **Positivity**

Negativity Bias dictates that we pay more attention to negative information than to positive.[5] Knowing this, we need more of an emphasis on what's right instead of what's wrong. What's working well instead of what's working poorly. What's been found instead of what's been lost. What's a strength instead of a shortcoming.

✓ **Principles**

When answers are ambiguous, we must honor our highest principles and make decisions from a place of values and integrity. Sometimes, this means doing things the best way, not the easiest way, and feeling short-term pain for long-term gain.

I have a favorite line from the movie, *Invincible*:

> **"CHARACTER IS TESTED WHEN YOU'RE UP AGAINST IT."**

OUTPERFORM THE NORM

In crisis, change and adversity, when you're surrounded by negativity, uncertainty, fear, apathy and discouragement, you have an open-ended opportunity to differentiate yourself by showing your true character as a leader.

Win the tug-of-war by amplifying your goodness.

SECTION 2

SHOW UP CONSISTENTLY

"Throw a bucket of water onto a rock,
nothing happens.

Let a drop of water fall onto a rock every day,
it creates a hole in the rock.

How impactful would you like to be?"

THE CRUX OF CONSISTENCY

"How is he today?" I ask, secretly fearing the response.

"Not good," replies Jared. "Best to keep your distance."

This was our standard conversation in between shifts at an upscale golf resort in northern Minnesota, circa 1999. Jared and I were "bag boys," which meant that we were responsible for helping members get ready to play their round and finish up afterwards.

Clayton, our boss, was in charge of the department. Some days were good. Some days were...not so good.

Jared and I realized early on that Clayton was a good guy. He had big, black glasses and a funny, dry sense of humor that caught you off guard at times. He had been working at the resort for over five years, since it opened. When he said something, you listened. I was always fine with that.

What we found most problematic was his consistency.

One day he would treat us like we were his best friends—very complimentary and caring. The next day (or, sometimes, even later that *same* day) we would get berated for not paying appropriate attention to members and not being fast enough with our service.

To use cheap golf puns, it "chipped away" at our belief in him as a leader. We *wanted* to work hard, but it was driven more out of fear than a desire to follow his lead. Even when things were going well, we were both on edge because we knew the "ball could drop at any point."

It created an impossible environment in which for us to thrive and be our best.

Consistency builds one of the most essential components in Outperforming leadership: TRUST.

Have you ever had a boss, manager, leader or coach, that acted erratically? How much trust did you have in that person?

I'm guessing not a lot.

It's natural that the two must work hand-in-hand for leadership:

CONSISTENCY IS THE RELIABILITY OF PERFORMANCE. TRUST IS A BELIEF IN THE RELIABILITY.

When we show up consistently, as our best, day-in-and-day-out, people know what to expect from us. It's dependable. It creates a psychologically safe place (see *Highly Effective Teams Have THIS*) for those that seek to follow.

That being said, I don't think anyone wakes up and says, "I'm going to act as inconsistently as possible today!" It's something that—often unwillingly and unknowingly—occurs as a response to things happening in our personal and professional lives.

So, it begs the question: How do we show up more consistently? Read on please...

WINNING THE MENTAL GAME OF LIFE

If you can win the mental game of life, you've won the hardest game there is to win.

Like an elite athlete, winning consistently is built on the basics.

In the Outperforming world, basics mean mindset. It's the foundation on which everything good, personally and professionally, is accomplished. The reason being:

THOUGHTS → FEELINGS → BEHAVIORS → RESULTS

These clichés are thrown around a lot, especially in self-help and personal development:

"Be positive!"
"Learn from your mistakes!"
"Have confidence!"
"Stay motivated!"

ALL of these things directly impact your results, which are impacted by your behaviors, which are impacted by your feelings, which are impacted by your thoughts (or mindset).

It's one thing to SAY you should have an Outperforming mindset. It's another thing to actually lead and GIVE someone the tools to bring it to fruition.

So, in the essence of moving from information to implementation, here are six simple ways to upgrade your mindset:

- ✓ **Surround yourself with GREAT people.**

Implement a zero-tolerance policy for people that don't support your goals, dreams and aspirations.

- ✓ **Feed your mind daily.**

Print books, eBooks, audiobooks, podcasts, TED Talks, videos—it has never been easier to consume positive content...if you choose to manage your inputs (see next tip) and make it a priority.

- ✓ **Contribute to others.**

It is really, *really* hard (if not impossible) to have a negative mindset when you know you're doing something good for someone else.

- ✓ **Be YOU.**

Stop comparing your performance to others and start comparing it to your own previous bests. Continuously improve. Grow. Evolve. Do it better than you did it before (see *The Best vs. Your Best*).

- ✓ **Celebrate your small wins.**

Stack 'em up! They're the essential stepping stones to big wins.

- ✓ **Laugh more, especially at your imperfections.**

There's enough seriousness in the world that embracing the fact that we're not perfect (and never will be) makes finding humor in every situation an exceptionally rare trait.

MANAGE YOUR INPUTS

You condition the mind like you condition the body. The same way that you don't get fit or unfit from doing one workout or skipping one workout; you don't adopt an Outperforming mindset by reading one article or listening to one podcast. It is something that happens repeatedly over time.

Many names have been used to explain this concept: *slight edge, compound effect, aggregation of marginal gains...*

They all describe the same principle. Performance is something that happens in small, almost imperceptible increments. The things we barely notice. This makes it even more paramount to consciously AND intentionally manage your inputs every day.

Inputs are the information you feed your brain. Outperformers know:

BETTER INPUTS PRODUCE BETTER OUTPUTS.
(PERFORMANCE)

As I'm writing this, we're about 12 days into the coronavirus and global pandemic. The coverage of the virus is EVERYWHERE. It is hard to escape it. I also know that I haven't helped myself—I have been guilty of spending multiple hours being consumed by what's going on locally, nationally and globally.

Almost all of the news is negative. It's updates on new cases and infections, death totals, lack of resources, a plummeting financial market, business challenges, etc. Finding positive information is akin to finding a needle in a haystack. It does not matter if it's you, me or Dupree; you cannot possibly be your best if those are the inputs you're putting into your brain for the majority of each day.

Now, you're obviously reading this because you're a leader (and, likely, a business leader). You may be thinking that it's critical to your business for you to stay up to date on what's happening in our society.

I get that. As a speaker who does 50+ live events per year, I have to stay up to date, too. This global pandemic has fundamentally altered my short-term business overnight.

But there is a distinct difference between consuming *enough* information to feel like you're knowledgeable and educated, and *so much* that you're fixated on it and it's no longer serving you.

I ask myself the simple question:

"WILL MORE INFORMATION FUNDAMENTALLY IMPACT ANYTHING THAT I'M DOING TODAY?"

If the answer is 'Yes,' carry on.

If the answer is 'No' (which it usually is), I don't need that unnecessary input. I'm good. I can move forward as my best self and proactively work my Outperforming day without it.

Always be conscious and intentional of your inputs. This is an extreme example during an unprecedented global crisis, but on a micro level, how you manage short-term inputs of information has a massive impact on long-term outputs of performance.

THE VITAL 4%

One hour is 4% of your day. It doesn't seem like a lot; but owning the first hour is key to Outperforming. It sets the tone for everything that happens thereafter. Consistency is built upon it.

What's the hardest part of anything in life?

Just. Getting. Started.

If we start each day from a static, standstill position, and get into immediate positive, forward motion, we have an excellent chance to sustain that direction for the entire day.

The morning routines of successful people have long been one of my fascinations. If there's one thing I learned in my research, there is no one perfect, blanket routine that works for *everyone*. Some people say to not open social media in the morning; others open Twitter before they've even gotten out of bed.

Still, here are four simple things that utilize the Vital 4% and truly set the tone for an Outperforming day:

✓ **Be Grateful**

When I ask the question, "what should we do in the Vital 4%?" to audiences, I typically hear responses like positive affirmations, meditation, prayer, devotions, etc. I refer to it as an Attitude of Gratitude (see *Attitude of Gratitude*).

In my estimation, we're all mostly talking about the same thing:

DOING SOMETHING PROACTIVE TO FIND PEACE AND PURPOSE IN WHY WE DO, WHAT WE DO.

The proactive part of gratitude may include a gratitude journal, in which you're writing down specific experiences that you're grateful for that day. Or it may be checking in, or doing something nice, for a family or team member.

If one of these proactive tasks doesn't resonate with you, *at the bare minimum*, I'd recommend a reactive way of feeding your peace and purpose.

The most popular reactive method that I've seen with Outperformers is listening to morning podcasts. It's reactive because you can be doing many different things, from exercising, cooking breakfast, commuting or curling your hair, while learning from world-class experts on ANY topic, for FREE. How amazing is that? Videos can serve a similar purpose.

The worst thing you can do, per the previous strategy of *Manage Your Inputs*, is to intentionally put negative information into your brain during the Vital 4%. I will not say that the news and general media are off limits; just be very conscious of what tone is being set for your day.

✓ Move Your Body

Exercise and quality movement is the single greatest performance enhancer for our lives physically, mentally and emotionally. NOTHING else replicates the benefits we get from exercise:

Physical	Mental	Emotional
Better Sleep	Cognitive Function	Self-Esteem
Immune Function	Mental Alertness	Happiness
Stronger Bones	Reduced Depression	Less Stress
Stronger Muscles	Mental Health	More Confidence
More Energy	Increased Focus	Boosts Mood
Anti-Aging	Brain Health	Less Anger
Better Posture	Productivity	Better Relationships

[6]

Shouldn't we, then, include it in the Vital 4%?

If you're not a "morning person," congratulations—neither am I! My girlfriend bounces out of bed every morning at 5:00am, excited about exercising, whereas I'm not excited about *anything* until I've had at least one cup of coffee ☺

My ideal time to work out is actually late afternoon. I find that it acts as a good reset between the day's and evening's activities. But I do know that it's A LOT easier for life to get in the way when you're planning a late afternoon workout. Fires come up and they need to be put out. There are less fires first thing in the morning during the Vital 4%.

Whatever this looks like for you, please move your body in the first hour of the day. I find myself doing many 15-20-minute workouts (usually while listening to a podcast) that include nothing more than getting my heart rate elevated, followed by stretching. Even if this isn't my "peak" time to exercise, I cannot deny that I have more Outperforming days when I get up and get it done.

✓ Fuel Your Body (and Brain)

Most people don't link what they put into their body and how it affects the way they think, feel and perform. From a "fueling your body" standpoint, this means your nutrition and hydration.

First, I'll readily admit that this is my own personal opinion and there's mixed research to support both sides of the argument, but I believe breakfast is the most important meal of the day and should not be skipped. Having *something* healthy (I'll usually opt for a nutrition shake) starts my day on the fast track to Outperforming.

What's not debatable, however, is the impact of hydration on performance. Because the body is made up of between 45-75% water and as little as 1-2% dehydration can impact mental alertness and cognitive functioning, drinking water and staying hydrated become essential.[7] My rule of thumb is to drink 20 ounces of water, *minimum*, during the Vital 4%. No exceptions.

✓ Plan Your Day

Brian Tracy, well-known business and success expert, says "Every minute spent planning saves ten minutes in execution. So, spending 10-12 minutes planning in the morning can save you up to two hours of wasted time and diffused effort."[8]

Regardless of whether this duration applies to your exact situation, planning your day will certainly save you *some* amount of time. And, that, is a good thing.

This was covered in-depth in the *Begin with Intent* strategy, so I'll simply reiterate two of the questions to ask yourself:

What would I need to advance to make it an Outperforming day?

SHOW UP CONSISTENTLY

How can I do this as efficiently, and effectively, as possible?

One other note—many Outperformers with whom I've worked like to "plan their tomorrows, today," meaning that they do the next day's planning before they leave the office. If this is you, continue doing it. That leaves even more time for gratitude, moving and fueling your body in your Vital 4%!

To close, owning the morning leads to owning the day. Whatever *your* current routine is for *your* Vital 4%, ask yourself:

> **"IS WHAT I'M DOING CONSCIOUSLY SETTING ME UP FOR PEAK PERFORMANCE TODAY?"**

Hopefully, it is.

REMAINING RESILIENT

I'm sitting at gate H11 at the Minneapolis-St. Paul International Airport. There's a young kid with big, curly blonde hair (bearing an eerie resemblance to a young Scott Welle) that is desperately trying to walk.

But he keeps falling down.

In fact, he's fallen down four times in the last minute. He's seriously struggling. If we assessed his strengths, there's no way *Walking* would be in his top 5.

I have to admire his tenacity, though. It would be so easy to quit, looking up and seeing everyone else walking around you, questioning why you keep falling and wondering when you'll be able to walk, too.

💯

At some point, you were this kid—a massive "failure." You fell down hundreds, if not thousands, of times.

But you got back up. You were born with all the resilience you need. You're an Outperformer, capable of handling hard situations.

"But, Scott, you're talking about a kid. I'm an adult now and the situations have much bigger consequences."

Bigger consequences than being able to WALK? I'm betting *that* was a pretty big consequence for you at the time.

OUR RESILIENCE COMES FROM THE PERSPECTIVE, OR THE LENS WITH WHICH WE SEE THE WORLD.

Here are the four common characteristics of highly resilient Outperformers:

✓ **Empower your Explanatory Style**

The foundation of resilience resides in your explanatory style, which is defined as, "our tendency to give similar explanations to different events."[9] It is, literally, how we explain the things that *have* or *have not* happened in our lives.

Psychological research has identified three questions to help you understand your explanatory style:

How much influence do you feel like you personally have over outcomes in your life?

Resilient people believe in their work ethic and abilities; less resilient people feel outcomes are out of their control ("bad things just *happen* to me").

> *How much do you feel like negative life events*
> *are permanent and fixed?*

Resilient people look at setbacks as temporary; less resilient people see setbacks as fixed ("bad things *keep* happening to me").

> *How much do you feel like one negative event*
> *will impact other events in your life?*

Resilient people think that negative outcomes are isolated incidents; less resilient people see negative outcomes as pervasive future failures in other areas ("bad things happen to me *everywhere*").

On the surface, these three questions might sound like common sense. But you've been using a specific style of explaining events, personally and professionally, for your entire life. Resilience stems from realizing the lens with which you explain your world.

✓ **There is no Failure; only Feedback**

The only way you can fail at something is to make a mistake and to not learn from it. Otherwise, we're all on the same journey of continued growth and progress, gathering feedback from our mistakes, trying to do it better the next time around.

**HIGHLY RESILIENT PEOPLE EMBRACE THE JOURNEY
MORE THAN THE DESTINATION.**

They find deep meaning in their life. If they encounter adversity, they ask themselves what lessons they're learning. They wonder *why this* instead of *why me*. They view setbacks as a setup for a comeback.

✓ Engage and Disengage

Stop trying to remove your stress! I've heard many coaches say, "you just need to have less stress in your life."

So, do you want me to go work in a toll booth? Or go lay on a beach and do nothing?

It's not about having less stress. In fact, I want you to be in the most pressure-packed, stressful situations possible. It means you're engaged in something seriously productive and worthwhile. What you need to do is strategically engage and disengage in and out of these situations.

Two things:

First, when I studied sports psychology, I worked with many golfers. It's a common misconception that a high-level golfer will be "on" for the 4-5 hours that it takes to play an entire 18-hole round of a tournament. In truth, they're *only* engaged when they start their preshot routine. Otherwise, even if they don't look like it, they're disengaged. Doing this allows them to effectively manage the pressure and stress of a round. This is a "micro-disengagement," and it can be something as simple as a quick break between meetings, a walk outside or a trip to the bathroom. Checking out, then checking back in, is a better way to manage the daily stress that chips away at your resilience.

Second, do something you find intrinsically enjoyable. This is a "macro-disengagement." It should be something that feeds your soul; something you love doing. Hunting, fishing, sports, concerts, plays, movies, art, or any other hobby, are all examples of things people commonly say are intrinsically enjoyable. Whatever it is for you, it's necessary the activity allows you to *fully mentally disengage* from the source of your stress. Scheduling time for this macro-disengagement, daily or weekly, will bolster your resilience and make you better when you do re-engage.

✓ Take Care of YOU

Bad habits almost always feel good in the short-term but are bad in the long-term. Drinking too much alcohol when you're stressed feels good as you're doing it; but feels bad when you wake up the next morning. Fast food and dessert taste great in the moment but can cause health problems and make you feel lethargic later on. Foregoing sleep to watch the latest docuseries on Netflix is fun at the time; but doesn't serve you when you're tired the next day.

Good habits are the exact opposite. You know they may not serve you in the short-term, but you're definitely rewarded in the long-term. This means taking care of YOU by monitoring your nutrition, hydration, sleep, stress and exercise is a key to sustainable resilience.

DAILY EXECUTION. EXTRAORDINARY RESULTS.

Goal achievement is simple. Not easy, but simple. Sometimes painfully simple.

Not long ago I spoke for a group of youth volleyball players. I don't do a lot of these speaking engagements, but I LOVE them...especially when the athletes are there to learn and genuinely want to get better.

I was kicking off their year and they were doing season-long goal setting afterwards.

All of them want to have excellent seasons, both individually AND as a team.

If there's one thing I've learned in 15+ years of working with high achievers in business and athletics:

OUTPERFORMERS FIND A WAY TO FALL IN LOVE WITH THE PROCESS OF BECOMING GREAT.

Not *being* great, which is an outcome; *becoming* great, which is a process. I asked them the following question:

"How many of you want to be great this season?"

Every hand went up.

I smiled as I responded, "That's what I thought. And how many of you would like to know a guaranteed way to make that happen?"

Once again, every hand went up.

"Here's what you must understand," I explained. "A season is nothing more than a collection of games, and you cannot be excellent in a season without being consistently excellent in your games.

Your games are nothing more a collection of practices, and you cannot be excellent in games without being consistently excellent in your practices.

Your practices are nothing more than a collection of skills and drills, and you cannot be consistently excellent in practices without being consistently excellent in your skills and drills.

So, if you really want to be great this season, **focus on being consistently excellent in each, and every, skill and drill you do.**"

As I scanned the players' faces, their looks were somewhere in between the shock of simplicity and the belief that there had to be something more.

There's not. This is, in fact, how you achieve greatness in *anything*. The consistent excellence comes from the attitude and effort you bring, which are both 100% controllable.

Want to achieve your annual business goals? This is a collection of quarters / months, which is a collection of days, which is a collection of your, and your team's, daily effort and needle-moving activities. Business goals are built on consistent excellence in your effort and activities.

Want to achieve a lofty fitness goal? This is a collection of benchmarks, which is a collection of days, which is a collection of workouts. Fitness goals are built on consistent excellence in workouts.

This book you're reading right now is nothing more than a collection of sections, which is a collection of chapters, which is a collection of pages, which is a collection of daily writing and research. Books are built on consistent excellence in writing and research.

In saying this, are you going to be 100% excellent every single day of your life? No. I won't be, either. Neither will your teams. There will be days that *you*, *me* or *they*, aren't as engaged. It happens.

As a leader, one of the best things you can do is to help your team fall in love with the process of becoming great. These daily attitudes and efforts, in isolation, mean very little. But it's the slight edge of stacking up consistent excellence over time that make or break lofty goals and worthwhile ambitions.

BE WHO YOU SAY YOU ARE

Have you ever met someone and realized they aren't who you thought they were? That your impression of them was different from reality?

It's disheartening. Deflating.

I attended a large business breakfast a while back where the speaker talked about leadership. His message was solid. It seemed genuine. Afterwards, I walked up to him to compliment him on his performance (something I like to do for speakers), but to my surprise, he couldn't have been more disinterested, dismissive and overall "too cool for school."

I was early on in my speaking career when this incident happened—and I'll never reveal the speaker's name—but it had a profound effect on me. I swore on that day that I would NEVER be a different leader on stage that I was off stage. My actions would always be consistent, and congruent, with my words.

> **WHO YOU ARE WITH ANYONE IS WHO YOU ARE WITH EVERYONE.**
> **HOW YOU DO ANYTHING IS HOW YOU DO EVERYTHING.**

Ironically, that next week, I spoke for a large group of project managers in Denver, CO. Three separate things happened that day:

First, I walked into a Starbucks across the street from the Denver Convention Center at 7:30am. As you can guess, it was PACKED. There were two separate lines for two separate cashiers. Like a grocery store, I picked a line and hoped it was the fastest.

I chose wisely (something that *never* happens when I go to the grocery store!), but after it became apparent that a customer in the slower line had chosen poorly, she, literally, started screaming at me, accusing me of cutting the line and saying I needed to wait my turn.

(the barista gave me my coffee for free because he felt so badly about it)

Second, I went to check into my room at the Hyatt later that afternoon, only to find out that my reservation (made by the conference organizers) had been made for the previous night. I didn't have a room. They also proceeded to tell me the hotel was full for that night.

Third, I was decompressing and having a beer with my girlfriend later that evening in a downtown pub. At the exact time that we should be leaving to make a dinner reservation at a nearby restaurant, our waiter has inconveniently gone missing. In the midst of trying to get our check paid, someone also walks up to our table that was in the audience that afternoon at the convention center. He wants to chat, in depth, about a few of the points I made and, basically, tell me his entire life story ☺

The point of these three stories?

BE WHO YOU SAY YOU ARE!

In my case, I cannot stand up on stage and talk about leading by example, having integrity, being compassionate, and caring about others if I'm going to turn around and yell at the Starbucks barista (or patrons!), the Hyatt receptionist and the restaurant waiter. I also cannot be too cool for school and dismiss an audience member for asking a question.

Please know, I'm not claiming to be perfect. I'm far, FAR, from it. I still get mad and impatient with people. But, when I do, I try to own it and do it better the next time.

We all experience these situations in our own unique ways; situations that test us and tempt us to not act consistently with our words.

Be who you say you are. Always.

SUMMARY GUIDE

Consistency is the reliability of performance.
Trust is a belief in the reliability.

Thoughts → Feelings → Behaviors → Results

Winning the mental game of life is the hardest game to win. Manage your inputs daily.

Leverage the Vital 4% with gratitude, exercise, nutrition / hydration and proactive planning your day.

Resilience comes from an empowering explanatory style, embracing feedback and not failures, strategically engaging and disengaging during your day / week, and taking care of YOU with good overall habits.

Fall in love with the process of becoming great. Consistent, daily excellence produces powerful long-term outcomes.

Who you are with anyone is who you are with everyone.
How you do anything is how you do everything.
Be who you say you are!

SECTION 3

BE COURAGEOUS

"To lead without worries, fears, judgments and insecurities is a heroic and courageous act."

ARE YOU AN IMPOSTER?

Sam slowly takes a sip of beer, staring at the bottom of his glass.

"I'm not ready," he claims. "No one thinks I'm an expert or an authority."

I respond calmly: "You sure about that, Sam? How many people have ever told you that you're not an expert or an authority?"

"Ummm...ahhhh...hmmmm...no one, I guess."

"So, Sam, is it really that 'no one thinks you're an expert or an authority' or YOU don't think you're an expert or authority?"

Sam has imposter syndrome.

> **Imposter Syndrome:** A collection of feelings of inadequacy that persist despite evident success.[10]

Feeling like an "imposter" is extremely common. In fact, many high achieving, highly successful people suffer from it.[11]

It's the employee that gets a promotion based on merit, but still doesn't feel qualified. It's the athlete that works tirelessly; yet attributes their success to luck. It's the parent who invests tremendous time and energy in their child, then struggles to accept compliments on what a great job they're doing as a mom or dad.

In Sam's case, he's been successful in corporate America for 20+ years. His knowledge, expertise and experiences are SIGNIFICANT. But he never internalized his own accomplishments, and thus, when he launched his own consulting business, he still felt like a fake.

If feeling like an imposter resonates with you, please do the following three things:

1. Admit it.

There's nothing "wrong with you" if you feel like an imposter at times. You're not weird. Or weak. Or broken. In fact, when Sam and I were having this conversation over happy hour, I readily admitted that I've suffered from this, on and off, my entire life. I still question why I should be the person standing on stage, talking to people about goal achievement, leadership, motivation, focus, resilience.

Who am I to be standing up there? Why would people listen to ME?

It becomes an if-then "chicken-and-egg" argument for all of us.

**IF I HAVE MORE EXPERIENCE,
THEN I WON'T FEEL LIKE AN IMPOSTER.**

**BUT FEELING LIKE AN IMPOSTER
KEEPS ME FROM HAVING MORE EXPERIENCE.**

In my case, I don't need more experience to get on stages; getting on stages is how I gain experience.

When I succumb to these uncourageous thoughts, I remind myself of the next point...

2. Let your Competence Fuel your Confidence.

If you suffer from imposter syndrome, there is a prosecuting attorney in your head, making a faulty argument based on insufficient evidence.

**MAKE A CONSCIOUS, INTENTIONAL EFFORT
TO TELL YOUR BRAIN THE TRUTH.**

In Sam's case, how many tens-of-thousands-of-hours has he spent working? Training? Acquiring and refining his skills?

So, grab the reins as the lead defense attorney and make a factual counterargument with the supporting evidence of your own competence.

Those late nights and extra effort got you the promotion.

That additional practice and conditioning caused your athletic success.

The sacrifice and attention to detail makes you a great parent.

Every single high achiever with whom I've worked has this reservoir of proficiency. We just need to remind ourselves of it.

3. No Failure, only Feedback.

Yes, this was mentioned in *Remaining Resilient* in the last section, but it bears repeating: a large part of imposter syndrome comes from the feeling of being found out; that you'll be exposed as a fraud.

This can ONLY transpire when you "fail." If you "succeeded," you'd never be exposed, right?

Anyone suffering from imposter syndrome must commit to the mental rewiring of never failing, of only getting feedback.

Fully embracing our abilities—whether it's an employee, athlete, parent or consultant—comes from setting the expectation that we'll make mistakes and perfection is not only indescribable; it's unattainable. Gathering feedback and trying to do it better the next time doesn't make you "lesser" or fraudulent—it is, in reality, the reason you're successful in the first place. All your competence has given you valuable feedback and lessons learned. Use them to your advantage.

FOR EVERYBODY = FOR NOBODY.

When I started writing my first *Outperform The Norm* book, I had "writer's block" for almost two years.

My biggest problem? I was trying to write something for everyone. And when you craft a message for everyone, you also craft a message for no one.

It's a common struggle for leaders: They simply want their message to resonate with too many people.

IT'S NOT EASY TO WRITE, SPEAK, OR LEAD, KNOWING YOUR VOICE IS GOING TO RUB SOME PEOPLE THE WRONG WAY.

A short time ago, I read an article about Minnesota Gophers' football coach, P.J. Fleck. Their football team has a long history of losing, but they're currently performing better than they have in the last 50 years. Fleck, a high-energy guy that truly "coaches people up," does an amazing job of maximizing the potential of his team.

There was one quote from the article that stood out: It was when he was asked about his leadership style:

"I'm not for everybody. And when you're a leader, you know you're not going to be for everybody. You have to be OK with not being for everybody when you're a leader. And if you are for everybody, you're not leading."[12]

Simple to say; not always that simple to do.

In Fleck's case, even though the team is winning, he has a lot of people that don't like him; that disagree with his approach. This is part of his secret sauce—it doesn't really matter if fans, media, or other coaches, don't align with his message.

What matters is that the message resonates with your team. If they are on board and follow, the team will Outperform.

Think about it like this: If you had 100 people in a room, would you rather?

- ✓ Have 100 people that are lukewarm. They aren't put off by you, but they won't necessarily follow you, either. They're marred by indecision.

- ✓ Have 50 people that are piping hot, and will listen and follow you anywhere, anytime. The other 50 people are frigid cold and want nothing to do with you.

Which leader do you think gets better results from their team?

I'm not saying this is easy. In fact, it may be one of the hardest things to do in leadership. But look at any great leader throughout history and you will find a somewhat polarizing person. Of course, the ideal is to eventually form a team with nothing but piping hot people towards you—the only way to do that, however, is to courageously convey your message. It cannot happen without it.

HANDLING HARD DECISIONS

A coaching client of mine had to make a hard decision. He was an executive of a large health club chain when the Coronavirus pandemic struck, and all the clubs were forced to close. With the immediate loss of revenue and an uncertain timeline for future reopening, he had a tough initial choice: continue paying loyal employees and risk putting the company in financial hardship or furlough 90% of the workforce, knowing that many of them rely on the income to pay their bills. And, if the second option is chosen, *another* hard decision is determining the criteria for the remaining 10% who "make the cut."

THERE IS NO EASY WAY TO MAKE A HARD DECISION.

No matter how much homework you do, how well you weigh the pros and cons and try to do the "right thing," it will still be hard.

Jim Rohn, one of my earliest mentors in personal development, said:

> *"Don't wish it was easier, wish you were better.*
> *Don't wish for less problems, wish for more skills.*
> *Don't wish for less challenges, wish for more wisdom."*

If you're in the position of needing to make hard decisions (most of us are), you've got all the strength, skills and wisdom to be able to do it. And, if you're prone to procrastination on hard decisions, realize that, by not deciding, you're *still* making a decision.

Following are five steps to consider the next time you need to make a hard decision. I won't lie to you and say it will be easier; but it will make it clearer on the correct path to choose:

1. Eliminate Decision Fatigue

We make thousands of decisions every day. Many of them are micro-decisions, such as what to wear, what to eat, etc. The accumulation of these decisions, big and small, cause decision fatigue over time.

If you have an extremely hard decision to make, *eliminate as many decisions as possible from your day*. Pre-determine what you'll wear and what you'll eat the night before. Delegate non-essential decisions. Move minor meetings to the future.

You want as much of your mental energy to go towards making your hard decision.

2. Prioritize Pertinent Information

We can all be guilty of paralysis by analysis, where we have so much information that it confuses us and leads to inaction.

Not all information is created equal. What is *the most important information* to consider in making your decision? In the earlier example, the company's financials are obviously an important piece of information, but so is the uncertain timeline of reopening.

3. Remain Logical

Being logical is easier said than done—human beings are emotional creatures. And because you have an emotional investment in your hard decision, this can cloud your judgment. Even if employees are temporarily furloughed, it's still better than the risk of the entire company closing, isn't it?

Most people will advise making a list of pros vs. cons, upside vs. downside, etc. Whichever method you choose to get the scenarios out of your head and heart, and onto something tangible (paper, screen), the better equipped you'll be to make a logical decision.

4. Strategically Involve Others

Is there anyone else who can lend outside, insightful input on your decision? At the end of the day, it is still YOUR decision, but seeking advice from people who have faced similar circumstances and challenges can prove valuable.

5. Avoid Catastrophizing

Have you ever built up something in your head, and when it finally happened, it was not nearly as bad as you anticipated?

We've all been there—it's called catastrophizing. It's an emotional false narrative in which we envision something far worse than it actually is (the present; making the decision), or the worst possible outcome of something happening (the future; the result of the decision). The advantage is that what happens is almost always better than what you imagined, but the emotional toll it takes on your psyche leading up to the decision can be immense.

BE COURAGEOUS

Also note that this differs from the "Don't Put Lipstick on a Pig" in *Crisis Considerations* because it's based on false reasoning, not logic.

Again, these five things will not make hard decisions easy, but they will put you in the best position to make them with clarity and excellence.

YOUR MESS IS YOUR MESSAGE

Leaders make mistakes.

That probably sounds obvious. You've made plenty, right? So have I. Inwardly, we know mistakes are how we learn, grow and develop. Here's the much harder part:

LEADERS ADMIT MISTAKES.

Research says that we're psychologically inclined to believe we're correct, even if there's overwhelming evidence to the contrary.[13] This discrepancy between our beliefs and reality creates "dissonance," and instinctively causes us to avoid admitting we're wrong.

But strong leadership and character are not defined by being infallible. It's quite the opposite, actually.

A long-term coaching client, Andrea, is a senior manager in higher education and is in the final round of interviews for a president position at another university.

In two weeks, Andrea was scheduled for the final on-campus interviews. These would make-or-break her candidacy. I could tell she was nervous, so I asked:

"What are you MOST nervous about?"

She responded, "That they'll ask me about something that happened many, many years ago and it'll be a huge red flag for them."

Andrea was referring to the fact that she never finished her dissertation in graduate school. She was going through a lot emotionally (including a divorce) and, personally, it wasn't a happy time in her life.

Even all these years later, you can tell she still carries shame and guilt from not finishing what she started.

My advice to Andrea?

"OWN IT. 100%," I said. "Not finishing that dissertation can be your biggest advantage and most powerful differentiator. That 'mess' can be your 'message.'"

Huh?

In my sales trainings, I talk about Psychographics, which is understanding, in depth, the attitudes, opinions and beliefs of your prospect or customer. In effect, this is what Andrea is doing—selling her to the university.

If you're in line for a promotion, or interviewing with a new company, you're in a similar position.

What is likely going through the minds of the university board members about the dissertation is: "Andrea didn't finish something years ago...I wonder how that's going to manifest itself if we make her our president?"

They're worried about history repeating itself, and I can't blame them. So, isn't it better to own it and address it up front?

There are three important factors when owning ANY mistake as a leader; whether it's to your company, organization, team or direct report:

- ✓ **Be Accountable.**

Accept, wholeheartedly, the results that came from your decision.

BE COURAGEOUS

✓ **Affirm Your Why.**

Give people a glimpse into your thought process and why you believed it was the correct decision at the time.

✓ **Emphasize What You Learned.**

State how it has made you an even better, more effective leader now.

In Andrea's case, here's an overview of the language:

"I didn't finish my dissertation and I own that. Unfortunately, I was going through a very tough time in my life and it's not a place that I ever want to go back to. But HERE'S what I learned from it and THIS is why it would make me the perfect president for this university in the future."

Andrea truly would be the perfect president. The interviews are for a smaller school, with students of lower socioeconomic status, and having a president that has struggled makes her even more relatable to the types of students she's leading.

Like Andrea, we all have moments we look back on—things we did or things we didn't do—and we feel shame, guilt, regret, weakness, or inadequacy.

All useless emotions that don't serve us in our journey to Outperform.

We think our mistakes are our largest liabilities. That they somehow make us inferior.

They don't. Leverage them correctly and they can be our greatest assets.

THE ALTER EGO

Cary Grant, an actor and one of Hollywood's leading men for almost 30 years, famously said:

"I pretended to be somebody I wanted to be and I finally became that person. Or he became me. Or we met at some point."[14]

Creating an alter ego allows you to tap into a better, enhanced version of you to handle a specific task.

Clark Kent created Superman. Bruce Wayne created Batman. Bo Jackson created Jason Voorhees. Beyonce created Sasha Fierce. Scott Welle created WELLE.

For all the athletes and top performing business leaders with whom I've worked, creating an alter ego is one of the fastest ways to boost performance.

To get this out of the way, I've spoken to hundreds of audiences and thousands of people about this concept, and a common question I receive is, "Scott, won't this make me look fake?"

I can fully appreciate from where the question comes.

But if your goal is to perform more courageously, let me ask you this: "What's the REAL version of you? Is it someone that holds back and potentially underperforms in specific situations?"

I doubt it.

> **AN ALTER EGO IS TAKING SOMETHING THAT IS ALREADY INSIDE OF YOU AND ALLOWING IT TO COME OUT.**

It gives you the opportunity to fully express the best, Outperforming version of YOU.

Much of the requirement for an alter ego comes from our earliest experiences and upbringing. We develop belief systems during these times—about authority, conflict, value, confidence, money, collaboration, etc. We ALL have them. These faulty belief systems simmer beneath the surface, and when we're put in specific situations as adults, they hold us back.

To rid yourself of these belief systems, you need to create a character, or persona, that doesn't operate this way (a different "operating system," so to speak). At the beginning of this process, you must do it as *them*; you cannot do it as *you*. Amateur coaches will tell you to "just go out and act more courageously." It doesn't work. You've been operating by your belief systems for your entire life. There must be a sharp distinction between you and your alter ego.

Answer the following three questions to get started on creating your alter ego:

1. What situations make you feel most uncomfortable?

The alter ego is not a global strategy; it's for *specific* situations. Common examples I hear are public speaking, negotiating value / price, having crucial conversations with employees and responding to adversity. We all have them—what's yours?

2. Who is a character or persona and how would they handle it?

Let your imagination run wild here. Your alter ego can be a comic book hero, a celebrity or something completely made-up and unique to you.

After identifying *who* this is, how would *they* handle the situation that makes you uncomfortable?

> *Mentally, what do they say to themselves? Dominant thoughts?*
> *Physically, how do they move? Stand? Look?*
> *Emotionally, how do they feel? Mood? Energy?*

How does your character, or persona, SHOW UP? The more descriptive you can be on these aspects, the better.

3. What's a trigger that you can use to initiate the transition?

Triggers are something that are ONLY paired with your alter ego—not used otherwise. It can be an article of clothing (shoes, belt, watch, glasses), a song you listen to, or a routine you perform (your breathing and how you walk into your "field of play").

Start in small spurts—no more than 5 minutes—by initiating the transition to your alter ego with your trigger. Do this consciously and intentionally. It may be difficult at first, but with practice, you will find it easier to make the transition. You'll also be able to stay "in character" for longer. Eventually, you and your alter ego will become one.

To close, I was recently doing a peak performance workshop for senior managers at Sherwin Williams' corporate office in Cleveland on this concept. A man raised his hand and claimed he didn't have any situations that made him feel uncomfortable.

(I've heard this before and it's rarely—if ever—the truth)

I said, "Really? There are no professional situations in which you'd like to perform better? Where you feel like you're holding back?"

After a bit of probing, he finally admitted that he feels very uncomfortable every time he has to meet with the CFO and CIO to report budgets, updates on projects and future initiatives. So, we started there and walked through the entire alter ego process.

I guarantee the next time he walks into a meeting with the CFO and CIO, he'll Outperform and be an enhanced, better version of himself. If you apply the alter ego process, you will be, too.

BE COURAGEOUS

For the full Alter Ego playbook, please access the bonuses at:
OutperformTheNorm.com/books

CRISIS CONSIDERATIONS

Following the financial crisis of 2007-2008, Ford was close to declaring bankruptcy. The American automotive industry appeared doomed and it's what most "insiders" expected the company to do. But what external people could not see was the change in leadership—bringing on Alan Mulally as CEO in 2006—and the internal influence it had over the people and principles at Ford. Mulally made thoughtful decisions and got the employees, at all levels, to dedicate themselves to a "detail to product" philosophy that, despite the terminology, wasn't so much about the products themselves—it was about the *level of care* by the people making the products. This dramatically changed Ford's market position, allowing the company to pay out $5,000+ bonuses to all hourly workers in 2011, the largest in a decade.[15]

During a crisis, a good leader can make or break a company, community or team. Every crisis is unique—and, with it, comes opportunity—but it is problematic because no definitive A-to-Z manual exists for how to navigate it.

That being said, here are seven crisis considerations to apply to your own unique situation:

✓ **Meet People Where They Are**

According to Maslow's Hierarchy of Needs, you're always going to default to the lowest level at which your needs are not being met.[16]

This means you cannot effectively speak to someone about the company's strategic plan if they're out stockpiling hand sanitizer and toilet paper.

You need to meet them where they are, which is acknowledging their fears by active listening and demonstrating empathy (see *A Different Pair of Shoes*) and helping them feel safe through structure (see *Un(certain)ty*).

"But, Scott, we're in a crisis! I don't have time for this—we need to move fast!"

Yes, I understand. I'm not saying you need to *keep* them there; but you do need to *meet* them there.

✓ **Don't Put Lipstick on the Pig**

Leaders in crisis need to accept reality; not only what is happening now, but what can potentially happen in the future.

Normally, I'm a heavy proponent of overwhelming optimism. In a crisis situation, however, you need to identify, and prepare for, the worst possible scenario. Is it bad? How much worse can it get?

**DON'T TRY TO PUT LIPSTICK ON THE PIG
IF YOU HAVE NO RATIONAL REASONING FOR DOING SO.**

If your team is in a fight; let them know they're in a fight. AND let them know if you're uncertain about when it will be over. Most people think, as a leader, you're supposed to have all the answers, but your team will appreciate the open, honest communication more than telling them what you think they want to hear.

✓ **Run the Unknown vs. the Known**

You have two sets of data to inform your decisions during a crisis: what you've seen and what you've studied. What you've seen is based on your own personal life experiences and what you've studied is your research, education and knowledge.

In your current crisis, can you find a close comparison to gain insight? Also, what lessons have you learned that you can draw from now?

✓ **Anticipate Aftershocks**

Anyone that has ever experienced an earthquake knows that when you think it's over, it's not actually over. There are always aftershocks that are felt well after the earthquake stops.

It can be very easy to bypass what's important and forthcoming during a crisis, in favor of what's urgent and critical. What are some "aftershocks" (consequences) that could be felt after the "earthquake" (crisis) is done? Taking a moment to thoughtfully answer this question will put you in a better long-term, stable position.

✓ **Rely on Others**

The natural inclination for many leaders during a crisis is to go into command-and-control mode, isolate themselves, and try to "figure it out on my own."

I understand why people do it—it's reinforced rhetoric in our society. We hear things like, "Franklin Delano Roosevelt personally led us through the great depression," and, "Steve Jobs single-handedly brought Apple back from near bankruptcy."

The reality is, they were the President and the CEO, *who led but also relied on a lot of other great people*, to navigate through their crises.

How can you empower your team to help in key decisions? Who else can you gather input from that has been there, done that? Where can you turn to for guidance and support?

Don't be Atlas, where you retreat into isolation and attempt to carry the weight of the world on your shoulders. It's one of the worst things you can do as a leader.

✓ Show Your Sacrifice

People will follow what you DO; not what you SAY.

A crisis often calls for sacrifices to be made. This may be compensation cuts, staying late or shouldering additional responsibilities.

SACRIFICE STARTS WITH YOU.

It's the very basis of Simon Sinek's book, *Leaders Eat Last*. When you, as a leader, make the sacrifice first, others will see it, embrace it and feel naturally compelled to follow suit.

✓ Leave No One Behind

Ask anyone who has served our country about the philosophies by which they live, and it won't take long before they say, "we leave no one behind." When said, it's not a boast of bravado and machismo; it's a mindset of deep humility and accountability. It's part of the Warrior Ethos.

A crisis is a battle and your team are your soldiers. Not only does this mantra provide inspiration, but it reinforces that you're all in it together and no goal is met unless it's met for everyone. Remind your team of this and you will, eventually, prevail.

THE ONE BIG QUESTION

According to Amy Morin, psychotherapist, we have 10 fears that hold us back in life:[17]

- ✓ Change
- ✓ Loneliness
- ✓ Failure
- ✓ Rejection
- ✓ Uncertainty
- ✓ Something Bad Happening
- ✓ Getting Hurt
- ✓ Being Judged
- ✓ Inadequacy
- ✓ Loss of Freedom

A solid argument could be made that, on some level, ALL of these things hold us back from acting courageously. We stay in a bad relationship because we fear loneliness. We don't take a risk because we fear something bad happening. We don't stretch outside of our comfort zone because we fear uncertainty.

Franklin D. Roosevelt famously said:

> "COURAGE IS NOT THE ABSENCE OF FEAR
> BUT RATHER THE ASSESSMENT THAT
> SOMETHING ELSE IS MORE IMPORTANT THAN FEAR."

OUTPERFORM THE NORM

This quote has always resonated with me, and a question I've asked myself, over and over, when I'm contemplating anything courageous in my life:

What else is more important than this fear?

A new, fulfilling relationship may be more important than the fear of loneliness.

A great reward may be more important than the fear of risk.

A next level of growth may be more important than the fear of uncertainty.

Personally, I had to overcome a fear of inadequacy when I wrote my first book. I didn't feel like I was "good enough" to be an author. Who would want to read *my* book, anyway? But spreading the Outperforming message was more important.

I had to overcome a fear of being judged when I spoke on my first stage. I thought everyone would critique and criticize me. But sharing my voice in the service of helping others was more important.

I had to overcome a fear of failure when I registered and ran 100 miles. I thought not getting to the finish line would be catastrophic. But being willing to try, and to put myself out there, was more important.

If you're EVER stuck in a spot where fear creeps in and courageousness is in doubt, ask yourself what else could be more important than the fear. If your answer is strong enough, you'll always triumph over it.

BE COURAGEOUS

SUMMARY GUIDE

Imposter syndrome is common. Admit it, let your competence fuel your confidence and resist seeing "success" and "failure."

If you're for everybody, you're for nobody.
Don't be a lukewarm leader.

There's no easy way to make a hard decision. Prioritize pertinent information, remain logical, strategically involve others and avoid catastrophizing.

Leaders don't just make mistakes; they ADMIT them.

Creating an Alter Ego is the fastest way to boost performance. It takes something already inside of you and allows it to come out. Use it to help you through uncomfortable situations.

Leading through a crisis requires meeting people where they are, not being overly optimistic, using data of what you've seen and studied, anticipating aftershocks, relying on others,
showing your own sacrifice *first* and leaving no one behind.

Courage is not the absence of fear; it's the triumph over it.

For the 5-part Courageous Leadership Series: Mindset, Messaging & Moving Forward, please access the bonuses at:
OutperformTheNorm.com/books

SECTION 4

COMMUNICATE EFFECTIVELY

*"Tell me and I forget,
teach me and I remember,
involve me and I learn."*

A DIFFERENT PAIR OF SHOES

In 2017, United Airlines made, arguably, one of the biggest corporate missteps in recent memory.[18] A full flight was boarded and set to depart Chicago O'Hare International Airport when additional crewmembers arrived, claiming they needed to be seated on the flight.

The flight attendants offered $1,000 in voucher compensation for any passengers that were willing to give up their seat. There were not enough takers.

Stuck in a difficult situation, the attendants approached a physician—who had paid for his seat—and told him, unfortunately, he needed to get off the plane.

The passenger resisted and was unwilling to leave. Eventually, Chicago Aviation Security was called in to physically remove the gentleman from the plane.

As if the visual of a paid passenger being dragged from an airline wasn't bad enough, the response by United Airlines' CEO Oscar Munoz only fanned the flames.

His first statement coldly read, "I apologize for having to re-accommodate these customers." The message lacked complete understanding for the passenger.

After moderate pushback, he compounded the error in his second statement by blaming the passenger, claiming he was "disruptive, belligerent and uncompliant." (keep in mind, this was a *paid* passenger!)

Now, fully engrossed in a complete PR nightmare, Munoz finally struck the right chord on his third try, saying "no one should be mistreated in this way and we take full responsibility," adding "It's never too late to do the right thing. I promise we will do better."[19]

It was a costly mistake for an initial lack of empathy.

Empathy is the ability to understand another person's experience, perspective and feelings. It's not niceness; it's understanding. Empathy is appreciating the effect your decisions and actions will have on others; a key competency of Outperforming leadership.

You may have heard the popular phrase: "you need to put yourself in someone else's shoes." That's only partially correct. You need to put yourself in someone else's shoes as *them*, not as *you*. If you cannot see *their* perspective from *their* shoes, all you're doing is wearing a different pair of shoes as you.

Like anything, there is a genetic component to empathy but much of it can still be learned. And, yes, you can have *too much* awareness of what other people are feeling and it can paralyze your decision making—though this is something I rarely see.

Type-A, go-getting leaders are typically great at sifting through large amounts of information and making quick decisions. As long as you can stop, consider and *care about*, how your decisions affect others and that *their* agenda may not be *your* agenda, you are well on your way to communicating effectively.

BE INSATIABLY CURIOUS

Two years ago, I spoke at a conference in Milwaukee, Wisconsin, and Bo Ryan was the closing keynote speaker. If that name means nothing to you, he was a legendary University of Wisconsin-Madison (my alma mater) men's basketball coach.

His impressive resume includes:[20]

- ✓ 747 total wins
- ✓ Four Division III National Championships
- ✓ Two Final Four appearances
- ✓ 40+ years in coaching
- ✓ 2017 inductee into the College Basketball Hall of Fame

To basketball fans, Bo Ryan is an icon in the state of Wisconsin.

I'd never actually met him because he was a coach after I'd graduated from the university, so when I heard that he was going to be the closing keynote speaker, I made it my mission to meet him. I had so many questions I wanted to ask him:

What's your philosophy on coaching?
How did you balance being tough and being caring?
Why were you such a great leader of young men?

My breakout session was earlier that morning and I found out from the conference organizer that Bo was going to be arriving shortly after I finished.

I strategically made sure that I was in the lobby of the Crowne Plaza hotel when he arrived. I immediately walked up to him, shook his hand and introduced myself (he initially thought I was a Crowne Plaza employee). I told him that I was here speaking at the conference.

"Oh, that's great. What did you speak about?" he responded.

I said that my session was about peak performance, leadership and productivity.

"That's really interesting. Tell me more about your company."

I explained that I work with business leaders and athletes to Outperform.

He leans in. "Wow, how long have you been doing it?"

I'm slightly caught off guard that he's asked every question and I've asked none. As I get pulled away to sign some paperwork, I tell myself that it's okay; there's still time.

About 5-10 minutes later, I see him in a break room, backstage from where he will be speaking.

But, now, I notice he has the conference brochure in his hand. He's read it cover-to-cover, including my personal and professional bio.

Before I can open my mouth, he asks, "You've really done Ironman Wisconsin five times?"

COMMUNICATE EFFECTIVELY

"Yes, sir. I have."

"How did you train for that?"

I give him the short answer of "A lot of swimming, biking and running," but, then, he asks me about my background in sport psychology and how I used that in my racing and business.

At this point, I'm getting frustrated. I'm thinking to myself: *You're BO RYAN, Wisconsin basketball coaching god! You've coached basketball for more years than I've been on this planet. What in the heck can you learn from ME? I should be learning from YOU!*

At that moment, it hit me. I realized this simple interaction with a hall of fame basketball coach told me everything I needed to know about why he was so successful as a coach and as a leader.

He's endlessly curious about other people, about the world, about how things work, about YOU.

Think of the great leaders you've had in your life—do they talk about themselves constantly? Do they act like they have it all figured out? That they've got nothing left to learn?

Probably not. You certainly know people like that, but they aren't the ones that impact and inspire you.

I heard John Maxwell, leadership expert, say on a recent podcast:

> **"I REALIZED EARLY ON THAT I COULDN'T LEARN A SINGLE THING FROM TALKING; I COULD ONLY LEARN BY LISTENING."**

That hit home with me.

It sounds strange that great leaders communicate effectively by being curious—but that's where it starts. They never stop growing, never stop listening and never stop asking questions to improve their own personal performance.

With curiosity comes wisdom, and with wisdom, leadership.

INTUITIVELY MAKING SOMEONE'S DAY

This section has purposely started with empathy and curiosity: two concepts that require active listening and the search for understanding. Both pave the way for intuitive reasoning and one of the most widely used tactics in decision-making:

"TRUST YOUR GUT."

There is a growing body of research that shows Outperformers, from Gary Kasparaov, the greatest chess player in the world, to Warren Buffet, one of the most successful investors in history, use intuition to unconsciously process large amounts of information and to make efficient, accurate, complex decisions.[21]

"Trusting your gut" is not just a punch line; it's backed in sound science and research.

But intuition also serves us for communicating effectively and recognizing the feelings of those around us. Highly intuitive leaders use unconscious processing to "gauge the pulse of the room." They know the right thing to say, how to say it, and when to say it.

For example, I recently presented for a group of managers in Edina, MN, on strategies for peak performance. At one point, when discussing resilience, I brought up losing both of my parents within 13 months, before my 38th birthday, and how challenging it was for me personally. Over the course of a two-hour intensive workshop, I probably didn't talk about this for more than two minutes.

Afterwards, I was signing books and chatting with people when an older gentleman approached me. With his white hair and glasses, he looked like Colonel Sanders, sans the bucket of Kentucky Fried Chicken.

He put his hand on my shoulder and said, "I'm proud of you."

COMMUNICATE EFFECTIVELY

At first it didn't really register what he was saying. I just looked at him, slightly puzzled.

In his intuitive, grandfatherly way, he continued: "You obviously love what you do and you're good at it. I'm sure with your parents being gone, you probably miss hearing someone say that they're proud of you. So, I want you to know that I am...and I'm sure they are too."

I've been fortunate to interact with thousands of people after speaking engagements and this was one of the nicest things anyone has ever said to me. Colonel Sanders almost made me cry! He made my day.

NEVER UNDERESTIMATE THE POWER OF A SIMPLE COMMENT OR INTERACTION AND HOW IT CAN MAKE SOMEONE'S DAY.

As leaders, this is what we DO. We actively listen to others, seek to understand, grow, and intuitively react to the situations around us. We read the room and know what people need.

Yet, how often do we have a FEELING that we *should* say something or make a definitive decision, but we don't? We fail to trust our extremely perceptive, unconscious processing gut, that, more often than not, steers us in the right direction.

EPP: EXPECTATION PERFORMANCE PROCESS

Assumptions: We ALL have them. We see someone that is black or white, rich or poor, democrat or republican, fit or overweight, and *we assume something about the person.*

OUTPERFORM THE NORM

To completely rid ourselves of assumptions is unrealistic—they are, literally, ingrained into our psychology based on our experiences and interpretations. The best we can do is to recognize when it happens and to not let false assumptions cloud our judgment and behavior.

A recent Wednesday night reminded me of this point.

I took an evening flight from Denver, CO, to Tampa, FL. I had run that day, at altitude, and the last thing I wanted to do was to show up in a warm-weather climate already dehydrated.

So, I drank water...A LOT of water. Throughout the 3 hour and 15-minute flight, I had five cans of Deja Blue water.

I was basically chugging it.

Because it was an evening flight, the cabin lights were dimmed. As we started our descent and I was coolly polishing off my fifth can, the lights came on. The lady sitting next to me took off her headphones and turned to me. We hadn't said anything to each other the entire flight.

"Oh, that's WATER in your can?!?!" she said. "I thought you were chugging BEER this whole time!"

I laughed hysterically, then responded:

"You really thought I hammered down five beers on this flight???"

She obviously did.

Now, please be honest—if you were sitting next to someone on an airplane and you saw them chug five cans of water vs. beer, what would your assumptions be about the person?

I'm guessing they'd be very different. Mine would be too.

WE ALL NEED TO BE COGNIZANT OF FALSE ASSUMPTIONS, ESPECIALLY IN LEADERSHIP.

It can be a huge blind spot.

These assumptions can affect the performance of others via the Expectation Performance Process (EPP).[22] To simplify, consider the following two scenarios:

1 – You identify Bob as a high-potential, long-term team member
2 – You identify Bill as a low-potential, short-term team member

Your "identification" of these people are based on your initial perceptions of them as a person, and of their behavior. After these perceptions, you develop expectations for what they are, or are not, capable of accomplishing. This, in turn, affects the quality AND quantity of your instruction and interactions.

You invest more in Bob and, because of this, he thrives and develops, thus confirming your initial expectations.

You invest less in Bill and, because of this, he stalls, disappoints and quits, also confirming your initial expectations.

Now, ask yourself: What if your expectations of Bob and Bill were flawed from the beginning?

This is the EPP at work. There isn't a fool proof way to defend against it, except to:

- ✓ Know it exists. Awareness is key.
- ✓ Be objective and impartial
- ✓ Start everyone with a clear, blank slate
- ✓ Use a fair meritocracy
- ✓ Invest in everyone equally (at least at the start)

We all have a leadership story in which someone saw something in us that we didn't, yet, see in ourselves. Because of this, we stretched ourselves, gained confidence and became something greater. What if the person's expectations had been different?

TO DELEGATE IS TO EMPOWER

Delegation is a critical—and often vastly missing—skill among leaders. In a 2007 study on time management, almost half of 332 companies were concerned about their employees' ability to delegate.[23] Worse yet, only 28% offered any training on effective delegation.

According to Harvard Business Review, a tell-tale sign that you're beginning to hoard work and resist delegation is if you find yourself working long hours and feeling completely indispensable to the company, while your team members aren't terribly energized or taking ownership; and seem to be working more regular hours.[24] It feels like no one cares about the company as much as you do.

This book is not simply about strategies and tactics—it's about the psychology underneath it. So, instead of discussing *how* to delegate; it makes sense to first understand *why* we don't delegate in the first place. These are the four standard reasons, complete with internal dialogue:

- ✓ "I will do a better job than anyone else"

This is typical of people with Type-A, perfectionistic personalities. Unfortunately, this becomes a vicious cycle. The more you do a job, the better you get at doing that job (and vice versa, for your undelegated team members), thus reinforcing the belief that you'll continue to do a better job.

The solution: Learn to give up control. If you don't:

**YOU WILL BE PERSONALLY RESPONSIBLE
FOR THE LIMITED GROWTH OF YOUR BUSINESS.**

Short of cloning you—and having an exact replica that can do the job as well as you can—there's no way to develop. There aren't enough hours in the day.

The skill of delegation is like a muscle, and if letting go of control is difficult for you, don't launch into a bootcamp workout. Start out slowly. Give a little, then observe and support team members as they go through the process.

✓ **"It's easier if I just do it myself."**

There's no shame in not being a great teacher. I'd volunteer that I'm in that boat. Doing it yourself seems like the *easiest* way; but are you sure it's the *best* way?

The solution: Play the long game of ROI. Usually, if it's "easier for you to do it," you're looking at the short-term return of performance for your investment of time. In the moment, you're right. You will likely do it better, faster and easier, than someone else.

But what about the long-term return of performance for the investment of time? If you (or someone else in your organization) could teach a team member to do a task, the more often that task needs to be completed, the greater return you're going to get on your delegation. *That* is what it means to play the long game.

✓ **"I need to prove that I can do it"**

Leaders in this category may not want to admit it, but their inability to delegate comes from a lack of self-confidence. They fear being shown up by someone else and made to look unimportant. Because of this, they shoulder an overwhelming amount of work to prove their worth.

The solution: This may be the hardest one to deal with from a psychological standpoint; there's a lot to unpack. Much of it is probably rooted in early experiences (see *The Alter Ego*). Ask the question:

"What's my end goal as a leader?"

Hopefully, the answer is to produce a *team* result that is something greater than anything you would produce individually. In the end, you will be celebrated as the leader, thus "proving" yourself to others.

✓ **"I like doing these tasks"**

If this is you, it's a good problem to have! It means you enjoy your job and that is no small thing. However, just because you *can* do everything, doesn't mean you *should* do everything.

The solution: Apply constraints. Ask:

"What can I do?"
vs.
"What can ONLY I do?"

It's the single best question I've ever heard in delegation. This question will help you to identify your most important, productive tasks and delegate the ones that are better handled by a team member.

Beyond these four typical reasons that people don't delegate, there can also be a fear of not wanting to burden someone by putting too much on their plate. This is easily combatted by using language of empowerment. Let your team member know that there are specific reasons you're delegating a task to them: *you believe in them, you trust them,* and because they're an 'A player,' *you need them* to deliver on this important task. They'll be empowered to do the job and do it well.

HIGHLY EFFECTIVE TEAMS HAVE THIS

In 2012, Google sought to answer a question: Why do some teams struggle while others Outperform? They embarked on a large-scale study of team effectiveness, called *Project Aristotle* (Aristotle, because "the whole is greater than the sum of the parts").[25] Beyond accountability, structure and team member value, the number one characteristic of highly effective teams?

Psychological safety.

Google defined it as "team members feel safe to take risks and be vulnerable in front of each other." I've asked the audience in hundreds of leadership presentations what dynamics make up the most effective teams and it's shocking how few people acknowledge, or are aware of, psychological safety.

IF WE ALL AGREE THAT THE WHOLE IS GREATER THAN THE SUM OF THE PARTS, PSYCHOLOGICAL SAFETY IS ESSENTIAL.

Why?

The team cannot Outperform if members are unwilling to ask questions because they don't want to be perceived as ignorant.

The team cannot Outperform if members don't openly admit weaknesses (or mistakes) because they don't want to be perceived as incompetent.

The team cannot Outperform if members don't offer fresh, new ideas because they don't want to be perceived as disruptive.

The team cannot Outperform if members don't challenge the status quo because they don't want to be perceived as negative.

OUTPERFORM THE NORM

It's common sense, but in the business world, it's rarely common practice. Mistakes are either hidden or openly criticized, innovative ideas are dismissed and discarded for "the way we've always done it," and leadership doesn't welcome constructive challenging of the status quo.

As a leader, you have the opportunity to do it differently. Implement these three things to create psychological safety on your team:

1. **Admit YOUR Mistakes**

As a leader, openly sharing your mistakes, weaknesses, lessons learned and vulnerabilities, gives people permission to share theirs.

2. **Welcome Fresh, New Ideas**

Reward people for being curious and challenging the status quo. This does NOT mean you have to implement every new idea that's suggested. In reality, you'll probably implement very few of them. But the quantity will bring out the quality, thus enhancing your team's effectiveness and performance.

3. **Give People a Voice**

There should be liberal pathways to leadership where people can be heard. Limit the rules and restrictions of communication, where "I'm sorry, but you can *only* talk to your manager or supervisor about that," and find ways to make each person feel like they're an active, valued member of the process.

Lastly, I recently did a training for a chain of dental offices outside Minneapolis, MN, on psychological safety. When I finished, I asked if anyone had ideas on how they could create more psychological safety in their business.

One person spoke up. "We should have a suggestion box where people can voice their thoughts, opinions and concerns."

It was a good idea and I wanted to reward the curiosity, but I also had to ask, "Would this be an anonymous suggestion box, or would you write your names on these things."

She thought about it, then responded, "Anonymously. I think it would be more effective."

Would it? Think for a second—if you have psychological safety in your workplace, why would anyone be afraid to share their thoughts, opinions and concerns, and to openly put their name behind it? There should be no fear of ignorance, incompetence, disruption or negativity.

The whole is always greater than the sum of the parts.

WORKING AND LEADING VIRTUALLY

Numerous studies have consistently demonstrated that the characteristics of the physical environment can have a massive impact on performance and productivity.[26] Even small, seemingly insignificant things that often go unnoticed—such as temperature, air quality, lighting and noise—influence our behavior. It's what makes virtual work problematic.

> **THE MAIN GOAL IN VIRTUAL PERFORMANCE IS TO NORMALIZE AN ABNORMAL SITUATION AS MUCH AS POSSIBLE.**

Working AND leading virtually are not easy tasks, but it is fast becoming the way the world works. Personally, I've been working from home for 10+ years, starting as a remote Regional Account Manager and now as an author, speaker and coach. I always pay close attention to what allows me, and my clients, to be more productive. Rather than resisting an increasingly virtual world, we must embrace it, and these are seven keys to help you to do that:

1. Dress for Success

If there's one thing I've learned, it's that you cannot be maximally productive in a hoodie and Zubaz. Actually, I don't own Zubaz, but you get the point…

Whatever you wear to the office, continue wearing it. Even if your physical location has changed, **wearing something that your brain associates with a given role or pattern of behavior will help your productivity.**

The most important article of clothing to wear at home? Shoes. It sounds strange, but unless you walk around the office in your socks, it's amazing what putting on a pair of shoes can do for your mindset. I'm convinced it has to do with the 7,000+ nerve endings in each foot.[27] When you put on a pair of "business shoes," your nerves signal to your brain that you mean business.

2. Create Boundaries in Your Spaces

Where will you work? If you have a home office, the answer is obvious. If you don't, decide where you'll work. This should be as clear as a certain chair at a table that you will only sit in when you're working.

Then, discipline yourself to only do work in this location.

WHEN YOU'RE IN YOUR WORKSPACE, DO WORK.

Don't work in bed. That's where you sleep.
Don't work on the couch. That's where you watch TV.
Don't work in the kitchen. That's where you cook.

Don't blur the lines. Challenge yourself, as much as possible, to *only* do work from one location.

If you have a family, this can also be used to define boundaries for them. Whether it's your kids or spouse, they'll start to understand and appreciate, that if you're there, you're working. They'll respect the space.

I understand many people that work virtually are thrust into unique situations, sometimes blurring the personal and professional lines. This will never be perfect, but it is a great way to maximize your productivity by being intentionally "on" in a certain location and "off" in others. Not only will you get more done when you need to, but you'll not carry the work over into other areas of your home, and life.

3. Set Your Structured Schedule

What is your standard work schedule? If you've recently started working virtually, do whatever possible to start AND stop at the same times as you normally would if you were in the office. Once again, we're trying to keep everything as structured and "normal" as possible.

The set schedule should not only be for the beginning and end of the day—it should also be for your meetings and calls. When will these happen for your entire team, for your project leads, for you 1-on-1's, etc.? Have a consistent, structured scheduled that you follow daily, weekly, monthly.

4. Have Clear Lines of Communication

When in doubt, a good rule of thumb for working remotely is to over-communicate with people. Because you don't have the luxury of seeing someone face-to-face in the office, if you think a person needs to know something, chances are they do.

Especially if you're a leader or a manager, also state clearly *how* the lines of communication should be used, i.e., team meetings are done via video conferencing, instant messenger is for quick check-ins, slack is for collaboration, email is for documentation and longer pieces of information. This clarity will help to keep the processes streamlined and effective.

5. Create a Virtual Water Cooler

The image of a bunch of employees huddled around a water cooler in the office, talking about sports or the latest current events, is a powerful image.

A VIRTUAL "WATER COOLER" COMBATS TWO OF THE MOST COMMON FEELINGS OF WORKING REMOTELY: ISOLATION AND LONELINESS.

These are loosely structured times that are not about strategy and business performance. Sure, the conversation might end up going there, but find unique creative ways that people can get to know one another as *people*. Virtual coffee, water cooler, lunch or happy hour are all popular ideas and I'd highly recommend doing it over video conferencing. This is the next best thing to actually being in the office together.

6. Simplify Your Systems

You want people focused on the work; not on *finding* the work.

Instead of 10 different emails and 5 different communication platforms housing important information, find a way to simplify the virtual systems as much as possible. Many times, this means not choosing the platforms that have the most bells and whistles. When it comes to simplification, often less is more.

7. Strike a Balance

Every leader of a virtual team needs to strike a balance between:

COMMUNICATE EFFECTIVELY

"Go be creative and autonomous."

and

"Fill me in on what's going on."

If you go too far with the former, a person may feel like you don't care about what they're doing. If you steer too far on the latter, you'll disempower them through micro-managing. It's a fine line.

This is something that's important to establish early on with a virtual team member. Ask for their input on the frequency of communication. It will obviously differ based on a person's experience; but making sure you're both on the same page from the get-go, will give you a starting point that you can tweak from there.

None of these strategies may seem earth-shattering but I promise they'll move the needle in the virtual performance for you and your team.

DEALING WITH DIFFICULT PEOPLE

When I'm doing leadership workshops, I have two questions that I will often ask the audience. First:

"How many of you have dealt with a difficult person?"

Every hand in the audience goes up. Some people will enthusiastically raise both hands! Second:

"How many of you consider yourself a difficult person?"

Crickets. Not one hand moves.

Isn't it funny—everyone has *dealt with* a difficult person, but no one *is* a difficult person? I'm not even sure if that's mathematically possible but it speaks to our perception of ourselves and our interactions with others.

The first fundamental principle to understand is:

DEALING WITH DIFFICULT PEOPLE IS ABOUT YOU.

No, I'm not saying you're doing something wrong or your perception is inaccurate, but it is on YOU to decide how you're going to respond to a difficult person.

Whether you're dealing with a person that is combative to authority, unclear on their expectations, prone to take credit when credit is not due, acts like a know-it-all, eats up your time with trivial issues or constantly criticizes, try these three things in your effort to deal with difficult people:

- ✓ **Listen and Stay Calm**

Many times, difficult people just want to be heard. They seek attention. The key is to listen *without the intent of formulating any response*. Often times, they're not looking for an answer. Acknowledge what they're saying and let them know that they're understood.

Next, stay calm. BREATHE. One of the worst things you can do if you are in an emotionally charged situation is to try to fight fire with fire. It's easy—and almost more natural—to see someone combative and to want to come back in a combative way. That's only going to cause more problems than it's worth.

Take long, slow, deep breaths and actively listen to the person. Patience is a key virtue in this circumstance.

✓ **Understand the Hidden Need**

No one was born out of the womb as a difficult person. There is an underlying, hidden need and, as leaders, we need to seek to understand what someone *really* wants out of a situation.

THEY'RE NOT BEING DIFFICULT FOR THE SAKE OF BEING DIFFICULT; THERE IS A REASON BEHIND IT.

Normally I would encourage using language like, "I understand where you're coming from," or, "I understand what you're going through." But, truthfully, if somebody is being *extremely* difficult, this can be the last thing they want to hear. They'll respond with, "No, you don't! You have no idea what I'm going through!" Difficult people are not always looking for empathy. In this case, let them vent and choose words such as, "I want to understand this better, please tell me more." As they're talking (and you're actively listening), seek to understand for what the person is actually looking. Do they want information? Affirmation? A sounding board? Autonomy? Safety?

Only through active listening can you truly uncover the hidden need.

✓ **Set Limits and Boundaries**

The first two strategies are more passive and the third is active.

Think of a difficult person that you've met; do you think they *know* they're being difficult? Almost certainly not. Most people lack the self-awareness of their own attitudes and actions.

So, *only after you've let them be heard and sought to uncover the hidden need*, when they're more receptive to feedback, bring it to their attention that what they're doing is not appreciated, or acceptable.

Be prepared for possible pushback at the start but stand firm on your limits and boundaries. You've let them be heard; you understand what they need. Bring their behavior to the forefront, through concrete examples (Important—critique the *behavior*, not the *person*!). Let them know how it's affecting you and others. You'll find, many times, people will be caught off guard by their own difficulty. They weren't even aware of it.

If you follow these three basic things, I'm not saying it's going to be roses and rainbows, but it will make dealing with difficult people easier and more effective.

PUT OTHERS ON THE PEDESTAL

"You're going back out there."

It was 6:38 p.m. on Saturday, June 7, and I had been running for over 12 hours—since 6:00 a.m. that morning—in the 100-mile Kettle Moraine Ultra Marathon.

Looking up, the hot sun still overwhelmed the summer sky...and showed no signs of relenting anytime soon. I sat—slumped—down for only the second time all day on a nearby picnic bench.

I was only at mile 63—and was lucky to have made it that far.

The last 15-20 miles had, to put it bluntly, kicked my ass. I was hot, tired and dehydrated. Everything on my body hurt, including my socks.

Physically AND mentally, I was a broken, beaten man.

Life is filled with defining moments and this was the defining moment in the Kettle Moraine Ultra Marathon. In a race in which more than 50% of the competitors will give up before crossing the finish line, there would have been no shame in giving up. The finish line may as well have been on another planet. It felt that far away.

COMMUNICATE EFFECTIVELY

As I sat on the picnic bench, I slowly lifted my head from my hands and turned to Diane and Missy, two of my good friends who had agreed to be my "crew" for the race and said, "I'm done. I've had enough."

They looked at me, paused slightly, and replied, "No, you're not."

I was not in the mood for a debate.

"Maybe you didn't hear me—I'm D.O.N.E!," I shot back. "I've already run 63 miles, which is farther than I've ever run in my life! I have nothing more to prove. Nothing left in my tank."

Impressively, they stood their ground.

"Scott, you've got this! You came here to finish a race and that's what you're going to do. You'll never forgive us if we don't make you try. You're going back out there!"

In every speech I give, I advocate surrounding yourself with great, trusting people if you want to Outperform. People that pull you up. And a criterion of this is:

LEADERS SAY NOT JUST WHAT YOU WANT TO HEAR, BUT WHAT YOU NEED TO HEAR.

At that moment of the 100-mile Kettle Moraine Ultra Marathon, I so badly wanted to hear that it was okay to give up; that I was validated in my decision to quit. Instead, I received a harsh dose of what I needed to hear; that I was selling myself short and was capable of doing more than I thought possible.

We ALL need these people in our lives. When I look at any accomplishment in my life that I would consider "significant" or "valuable," not a single one happened without being surrounded by great individuals.

It is *because* of others that I succeed. No one Outperforms alone.

I can honestly say that, if it wasn't for Missy and Diane, I wouldn't be a 100-mile finisher. I would have given up. I finished the race in 21 hours and 6 minutes, taking 14th place in my first (and, likely, only!) ultra marathon.

As leaders, we need to believe in others when they do not believe in themselves. I'll always be grateful to the people who have done that for me.

They deserve to be put on the pedestal.

SUMMARY GUIDE

Be insatiably curious about others. It draws them to you.

Trust your gut. There's science and research in why you should.

False assumptions influence expectations, and thus, performance.

Delegation is a difficult skill in leadership. When done right, it empowers others. When done wrong, it limits growth.

Psychological safety is the foundation of highly effective teams. To instill it, admit your mistakes, welcome fresh, new ideas and give people a voice in processes and procedures.

Virtual leadership can be enhanced by dressing for success, creating boundaries in spaces, structuring your schedule, using clear lines of communication, having a "virtual water cooler," simplifying systems and striking a balance between autonomy and reporting.

Dealing with difficult people is about you. Listen and stay calm, understand the hidden need and set limits and boundaries.

When you succeed, put others on the pedestal.

For more strategies on building psychological safety, please visit:
OutperformTheNorm.com/books

SECTION 5

CONNECT TO A PURPOSE

"Life is short.
Do something that feeds your mind & fills your soul."

THE REASON BEHIND IT ALL

"Mary, I have no idea what to say."

"Don't worry about that," she responds. "It's just a really tough time in the industry and a lot of people are losing money every day. They need inspiration and positivity right now, and help staying focused on their goals." The pain in Mary's voice is palpable.

It's early March and I've been asked to speak for the DHIA, or "Dairy Herd Improvement Association." I'm from small town, Minnesota, and I'm certainly familiar with farm life—but I never actually *lived* on a farm. Growing up, when I had sleepovers with friends who did, I thought it was "fun" to help them with chores in the pre-dawn morning. I didn't realize the fun quickly ceased with the mandatory obligation of doing these chores every day.

I have tremendous respect for farmers, and I wanted badly to help, but the prospect of speaking to the DHIA has me feeling like a fish out of water. The week before I'm keynoting a global leadership conference in New Orleans; this event would be at the VFW in Little Falls, MN. The audiences couldn't be more different.

I confess, "Mary, I'm not sure that I'm the right guy. I don't know the first thing about dairy or farming or agriculture or *anything*. What are you hoping to accomplish with the event?"

"Scott, our hope is that no dairy producer in our county commits suicide this year."

Wow, I thought. *That's heavy*. I'm caught completely off guard.

In that same moment, a seismic shift happens. The push to speak at an event becomes a pull to serve. The discussion of whether to show up is over.

"I'm in, Mary—whatever you need. Let's reconnect your people with their purpose."

CONNECT TO A PURPOSE

💯

A purpose is where you are; it's why you exist. If a vision is where you're *going*, a purpose is what you're *doing*.

It is what gets you up in the morning.

When you identify your powerful purpose, you willingly start earlier, stay later, and work more diligently for no other reason than you *must* do it. And you must do it not because someone else is telling you; but because you're telling yourself.

Companies define why they exist through their mission statement, and in the best organizations, everyone buys into it. But these are macro-missions; each individual team member also has a micro-mission, or their own personal reason(s) for what drives them to show up and Outperform.

I've noticed two common errors from my own experiences, and from working with hundreds of people on their purpose:

- ✓ **They've never taken the time to write it down.**

It's like goal setting—getting it out of your head and onto paper makes your purpose tangible. It makes it real.

- ✓ **They lose the connection to their purpose.**

It is not that you need to *find* your purpose—like you've lost your car keys or phone—it's simply something that gets unplugged and disconnected in the daily grind of life.

If you've ever gone through a period in your life where things feel "stale," or "blah," like you're going through the motions and not fully engaged in what you're doing, you've likely lost the connection to your purpose.

A purpose should be a strong string pulling you in a forward direction; but it doesn't work if the string has been cut.

The reason connecting—and *staying* connected—to a purpose is so rare, for companies and individuals alike, is that it requires a thoughtful, proactive approach in a mostly thoughtless, reactive society.

Here are some common examples of what people list as their purpose in life:[28]

- ✓ Solve problems
- ✓ Make positive connections with others
- ✓ Make things
- ✓ Leave the world a better place
- ✓ Empower others and lift them up
- ✓ Provide for my family
- ✓ Be successful

What gets *you* up in the morning? Is it one of these things or something completely different?

In the case of my agricultural friends, there are powerful purposes in carrying on the familial legacies of farms. There's also the pull to provide for their community, and to do what's right for mother earth.

As you conceptualize your reason for doing what you do, keep in mind that your purpose is YOUR PURPOSE. Define it, connect to it, let it drive you.

WHAT DO YOU DO?

If we met at a networking happy hour and I asked you, "What do you do?" how would you respond?

It's a simple question with a not-so-simple answer.

If you're like most people, you'll state your position or title, followed by listing your products, programs or services.

CONNECT TO A PURPOSE

"I'm the Chief Development Officer for a mid-size wealth management and financial services company."

It's a common answer—and it's not wrong—but is that really what you DO?

<u>100</u>

"Your job must be great. There's such purpose in what you do."

Bill discloses this to me at a National Leadership Development Conference in Hinckley, MN. Both of my presentations were earlier that day, but I stayed to attend other sessions at the conference and mingle with some of the sponsors, speakers and attendees.

We've been socializing late, late into the night (hey, I get to have fun too!), and in between bowling and singing, I found myself in a conversation with Bill, an external auditor, who readily admits that he had built up some "liquid courage" and is saying things to me that he never would have after my sessions.

Bill claims that it "must be so great to be me" because there's such purpose to my profession and he wasn't finding a lot in his.

I state strongly, "Bill, there's a powerful purpose in EVERY profession. You just need to connect to it."

When I ask him what he does, Bill responds, "I do external auditing."

"Yep, I get that, Bill. But what do you DO?"

"Well, I audit systems and operations for clients...and recommend improvements."

We're getting warmer. He's on the right track.

"Got it, Bill. So, what do you *really* DO??? Meaning, if you don't show up and audit with excellence, what happens to your clients?"

The best-case scenario is his clients don't perform to their fullest potential. The worst-case scenario; they go to jail.

What Bill DOES is give his clients safety and security, and peace of mind knowing they're performing at their organizational peak.

They *need* Bill. He's a *vital* part of their process. He has *purpose*.

Thinking on this level is a key component to motivation, employee engagement and peak performance. Instead of the surface; it's about the meaning. Instead of the logical; it's about the emotional. Instead of what you say you do; it's about what you actually DO.

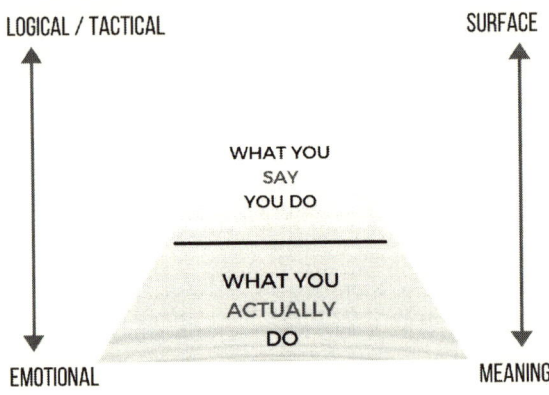

Peak performance and motivation are a psychological onion that requires peeling back the layers to connect powerfully to your purpose. It is how you raise psychological necessity and make it a must.

MAKING IT A MUST

You don't *have to* show up at the gym, for your team, at your company or with your family. Right? The world *will* go on if you don't bring your best.

So, why do you?

More importantly, why do some people make showing up as their best a *must* vs. a *preference*?

The answer is psychological necessity.

CONNECT TO A PURPOSE

Brendon Burchard first coined this term in his book, *High Performance Habits,* describing psychological necessity as "associating a deep sense of identity with performing with excellence."[29] When you do this, you take actions that are congruent with your identity.

I try to work hard
vs.
I'm a hard worker.

I want to stop smoking
vs.
I'm not a smoker.

I like to run
vs.
I'm a runner.

I strive to lead others
vs.
I'm a leader.

One is attempting to take actions as your current self; the other is associating a deep sense of identity within you and letting that guide your behaviors.

Do you *see* yourself as someone that performs with excellence?

The reason this is included in *Connect To Your Purpose* is because it drives how you show up every day and the excellence with which you do it. It is critical; like air to the lungs.

If you're leading a company, organization, team or family, what's your identity? WHO ARE YOU, on the most basic psychological level?

> **IDENTITY IS A STEP DEEPER, BEYOND YOUR VALUES.
> IT IS WHO YOU ARE.**

The words you're reading on this page came from the fact that I transitioned my own thinking from, "I'm trying to write a book," to "I'm a writer." Now, when I don't feel like writing, I still must do it because I'm a writer. It's necessary that I write and do it with excellence.

As a leader, this is an important distinction for you to use with your teams. Instead of:

"We want to have excellent customer service,"
say,
"We serve our customers with excellence."

Serving your customers with excellence is who you are; it's why you exist.

It sounds subtle but the shift in identity is essential to consistent, purposeful performance.

MANUFACTURING URGENCY

Lots of people teach productivity tips like keeping a clean desk, making a to-do list and having a "zero inbox" by Friday afternoon, but there is one purposeful game-changing strategy that almost no one talks about:

Manufacturing urgency.

Think about a time when you had a seemingly impossible timeframe to complete a task, whether it was cleaning your house for a holiday party, completing a term paper in college or crafting a presentation for a client. Whatever needed to be done, you got it done, right? Why?

You might be quick to say that it was because of a deadline. That surely created an external form of urgency, but have you ever missed a deadline? We all have, at some point. So, if the *deadline* was really the reason you got your seemingly impossible task done, wouldn't this apply universally to all situations that included one?

Something else is at work here. An internal form of urgency (to complement an external form) was also present.

If you want to fuel your, or your team's, daily urgency at any point, so they get more done, faster, consider doing these three things:

✓ Clarify the Consequences of Inaction

We are biologically hard-wired to respond more to feelings of pain and loss than we are to feelings of pleasure and gain.[30] If you don't take action on what you know needs to be done (but you may not be doing it), what will that cost you? What will it cost the team? What specific pain will you experience because of it?

The more vivid you can make this illustration, the better. Could you lose the business of your top customers? Be exposed as the weak link in your company? Not be able to meet a project deadline? Miss out on a bonus?

Yes, much of this is fear-based rhetoric ("if we don't do *this*, then *that* will happen") and, as a leader, I don't recommend using it as your dominant type of motivation, but it will lead to a short-term spike in urgency.

✓ Select the Causes of Complacency

What is the root cause of you not taking more urgent action? Assuming that the team understands the purpose and the importance of what you're doing, more often than not, this is due to "social loafing."

Max Ringelmann introduced social loafing as the psychological phenomenon of low performance and reduced productivity when one works in a group vs. when one works alone. He demonstrated this through a series of rope pulling experiments, finding that as group size increased, people's effort decreased. Eight people, he found, didn't even pull as hard as four individuals.[31]

The way you combat social loafing is twofold:

First, if possible, reduce the size of your teams. If you have a large team, consider creating sub-teams. Eight people should be the maximum size, with teams of 4-5 people being the sweet spot.[32] The idea is that this number is small enough to minimize social loafing but large enough to still be an effective team.

Second, have transparent and clear feedback mechanisms. In the rope pulling experiment, it's proposed that if every individual's effort (how much they were pulling) was *measured* and made *publicly available*, social loafing would be minimized. This principle has to be nuanced in the business world, but finding a way to tangibly represent the personal contribution to a team's performance facilitates urgency.

✓ **Celebrate Small Wins**

Lofty business goals are never achieved in a day, week or month, and it's hard to have urgency towards something that feels exceptionally far away. Some can do it; most cannot. It is becoming more glaringly apparent in our society of instant gratification.

HAVE MICRO-GOALS AND CREATE REWARDS FOR THEIR ACCOMPLISHMENT.

When I ran 100 miles, my single greatest mental strategy to keep the urgency of moving forward, was to focus on getting to the next "aid station" 2.5-4 miles away. When I got there, I would stop, reward myself by eating and drinking, then cross it off the list and turn my attention to the next aid station. I knew if I could rinse and repeat that approach enough times, I would arrive at the impossibly far away finish line.

As a leader, whatever you can do to show that you've made visual, positive progress towards something every day or week—no matter how small—will give you more belief in what you're doing, and thus, help you to take more purposeful future action.

MEETINGS THAT MATTER

Are you bored? Hold a meeting!
Lonely? Hold a meeting!
Hungry for donuts? Hold a meeting!

Research has shown that the number of meetings has doubled between 1960 and 1980 and the average senior manager spends 23 hours in meetings each week.[33] That's over two workdays each week spent in meetings!

Meetings are everywhere and they don't seem to be waning anytime soon.

One of the most common criticisms I hear from the organizations with which I work, is ineffective meetings. There's a real pain and consequence to the wasted time spent in meetings, namely lost productivity and performance.

AS A LEADER, IT'S TIME TO QUIT THE MEETING MADNESS.

Here are six steps to hold meetings that matter:

- ✓ **Have Crystal Clear Outcomes**

I have a question that I ask at the start of every meeting:

"What specifically are we hoping to accomplish in this meeting?"

I don't say it arrogantly, or condescendingly; it's a way for both of us to clearly define our outcomes from the outset.

"Discussing," or "hearing about" something is not an outcome. That's a process; a method you use to arrive at a destination.

If you know where you're going, you'll arrive there much faster.

When I asked this question at a meeting with a home mortgage company last week, they responded, "To give you insight into our business performance and identify a theme for when you speak at our 2020 Sales Rally."

That is an example of a meeting with a crystal clear outcome.

✓ **Send the Agenda in Advance**

Always send the meeting agenda, and any other pertinent information, in advance. Even if attendees are only able to glance at it beforehand, it still "primes" the brain for what's coming via unconscious processing (see *Intuitively Make Someone's Day*), thus making your meeting more efficient.

Also, whatever time frame you use for sending the agenda, stick to it. Whether it's a day or an hour in advance, it creates a repeatable routine.

✓ **Cut the Meeting Time in Half**

The last chapter, *Manufacturing Urgency*, described the impact of external deadlines on efficiency and performance.

IF YOU WANT TO HAVE MORE EFFICIENT MEETINGS, CUT THE TIME IN HALF.

"But, Scott, we'll never be able to get through everything we need to."

You may be right. But you may be wrong, too. You'll never know if you don't try. At the bare minimum, you'll be shocked at how much more efficient you become by constraining your deadlines.

✓ **Determine if you MUST be there**

Time is a zero-sum game. That means, whatever time you spend in meetings, is lost and cannot be applied to another task. This holds true not only for you, but for everyone else in the meeting. It's how companies have identified one weekly meeting that took up 300,000 hours a year.[34]

Ask yourself, "Must I be there?" If the answer is anything other than a definitive "YES," it's worth it to reconsider. Attending meetings is not a badge of honor; productivity and performance, is.

✓ **Minimize Participants**

Jeff Bezos has a "two pizza rule:" If two pizzas can't feed the entire group, then there are too many people in the meeting.[35] It's the method he uses to improve productivity and usefulness, and to decrease social loafing.

MEETINGS ARE NOT SPECTATOR SPORTS.

If you don't have an active role in the meeting, could you potentially send someone else and have them debrief you afterwards, saving you significant time?

✓ **End with Accountability & Responsibility**

A short time ago, I heard a Global VP of Human Resources in a Fortune 500 company cringe, when describing their inefficiencies: "We seem to think the goal of a meeting is to schedule *another meeting*. It's maddening!"

When Outperformers adjourn a meeting, they know WHO is responsible for WHAT, and by WHEN. They end with individual action items, and a plan, from the meeting that is rarely, if ever, to schedule another meeting.

If you're part of a larger culture where more meetings are the mantra, I understand this may be a tough nut to crack. Start by using these six keys with your team and take small steps. Once it shows up in increased productivity and performance, efficiency and effectiveness, it will be hard to debate the philosophy of only having meetings that matter.

ADOPT A RALLYING CRY

In 2017, I did a one-year Outperform contract with a division of a global medical device company. They had been underperforming for years and it wasn't going to be an easy, or quick, turnaround. Even though things were trending in the right direction to start the year, the progress wasn't fast enough for the leaders of the company. In June, the sh*t hit the fan. They imposed massive changes, including restructuring, resources being cut, discontinued product lines and an overhaul of the sales compensation plan. As this was happening, the president of the division was also replaced.

The teams were tasked with still finding a way to Outperform in the back half of the year. One team, the North Central Region, adopted a "rallying cry" based off of an old Ray Lewis (hall of fame linebacker for the Baltimore Ravens) video, called *Pissed off for Greatness*.

When resources were cut, the team looked at each other and said, "It doesn't matter, we're *pissed off for greatness*." When product lines were discontinued, same thing. When there was unstable leadership at the top of the division, they summoned Ray Lewis.

They used a rallying cry to define, unite and strengthen their team. It didn't matter what they went through; they were *pissed off for greatness*. At the end-of-year awards banquet, they proudly stood on stage, having DOMINATED the other regions in sales revenue, growth and overall performance.

One of the fundamental differences between a team, and a group of individuals, is that a team has something that makes them distinct AND unique. Something that sets them apart. You see it everywhere in sports — from a special team dance, an exclusive piece of apparel or a team rallying cry.

> **A RALLYING CRY CREATES A SINGULAR IDENTITY, OR SOMETHING THAT TRULY BONDS A TEAM TOGETHER.**

To be clear, a rallying cry is something that people say in the "locker room," or behind closed doors. It is not for public consumption. It's probably not your purpose (mission) or where you're going (vision), and it almost certainly is not something you're going to post on your website. It's a phrase, internally, when you're going through periods of good, bad and otherwise, in which your people will turn to each other and say, "remember our rallying cry."

This is the perfect exercise to do at an annual planning meeting and it *should not* be top down. Present your leadership goals and objectives, then task your team with coming up with a rallying cry that you'll return to throughout the year. Have them vote on which one they like best. This will give the team ownership over it and make them feel as though it's theirs.

A few rallying cries I've heard from companies with which I've worked:

> *The only way is through.*
> *Get sh*t done.*
> *Better together.*
> *Play to win.*
> *It's your job.*

Whatever rallying cry you choose; I guarantee it will strengthen your team and improve their performance.

CREATING A CULTURE OF EXCELLENCE

Corporate culture and strategy are separate but symbiotic. Culture will either contribute to or undermine strategy. In fact, while there are a lot of things the company can do to drive growth, the one thing that will directly impact everything else is culture. Corporate culture is the human performance engine that drives the level of success, or failure, for every business strategy, revenue initiative, operational performance and change transformation. Culture is a precursor and top contributing factor to anything and everything that requires employee effort.[47]

Books will be written about the New England Patriots' football program someday. I'm not a personal fan of the team but I respect their organizational excellence—six Super Bowl championships, 16 AFC East Division titles in 20 years, 17 consecutive years of winning at least 10 games. These statistics will never be duplicated.

Every year, multiple teams try to create the same level of success by copying a similar playbook in practices and games as the New England Patriots. It doesn't work. The "Patriot Way" is a culture of work ethic, attention to detail, doing your job, WE before ME, and perhaps most importantly, the deep-seeded belief that, regardless of what is happening, *they will win*.

THIS is the culture that drives their results.

COMPETITORS CAN COPY A PROCESS AND STRATEGY, BUT IT IS ALMOST IMPOSSIBLE TO COPY A CULTURE.

Lot of companies fly airplanes; not many of them do it like Southwest Airlines. There are plenty of tech startups but few of them are Google and Facebook. I can buy shoes from hundreds of online stores, but I can see, and feel, something culturally different with Zappos.

A culture includes an organization's vision, values, norms, systems, symbols, language, assumptions, beliefs, and habits. It's the overarching umbrella under which everything else falls, and is why Peter Drucker famously said, "Culture eats strategy for breakfast." Sometimes, many would argue, for lunch and dinner, too.

One of the most difficult things to do in leadership is to construct an Outperforming culture. It can be a pain-staking incremental process that doesn't happen overnight. But, when you have it:

AN OUTPERFORMING CULTURE IS YOUR MOST VALUABLE ASSET. IT IS YOUR GREATEST COMPETITIVE DIFFERENTIATOR.

To simplify what can often be looked at as a very complex concept, here are five important things to remember as you lead and construct your culture:

✓ **Clearly Define the Core Values in Your Culture**

What are the core values that you would like to embody your culture? I've already named some of the New England Patriots' core values. Zappos lists these 10 on their website:[48]

1. *Deliver WOW through service*
2. *Embrace and drive change*
3. *Create fun and a little weirdness*
4. *Be adventurous, creative, and open-minded*
5. *Pursue growth and learning*
6. *Build open and honest relationships with communication*
7. *Build a positive team and family spirit*
8. *Do more with less*
9. *Be passionate and determined*
10. *Be humble*

Your culture is your culture; it can represent anything you want it to. But it must be clearly defined. Whether it's comprised of 3, 5 or 10 components, it provides the essential compass from which you'll chart a forward direction.

✓ Audit and Align People Within It

Once you define your culture, people will fall into one of three categories: they fit the culture, they can be coached to fit the culture, or they're not in the culture.

Making this determination clearly, and swiftly, is a hallmark of great leadership. A culture is only as strong as its weakest link; everybody must buy in.

✓ Build Congruency in Your Actions

Southwest Airlines' culture is built around being happy and friendly. To embody this culture, the company gives their employees permission to go the extra mile to make customers smile. This includes dancing at the gate, telling jokes over the intercom and singing happy birthday to an unknowing passenger (all things I've personally witnessed). By doing this, it anchors in that their culture isn't just something that is *preached*; it's something that's *practiced*.

Whatever core values you decided upon for your culture, use concrete actions to demonstrate its importance. Also, give team members the autonomy to act out the core values.

✓ **Quantify Your Results**

What metrics will you use to quantify whether your culture is working? Standard business results are easy to do—gross revenue, profitability, market share, etc. But, especially if you're trying to change a culture, there is often a lag time from the implementation of a fresh, new culture and its true impact on organizational performance.

Are there other ways to quantify what you're doing, perhaps through surveys (internally and/or externally), group or individual discussions? Data from these "soft metrics" can act as the positive precursor to the more "hard metrics" listed above.

✓ **Celebrate and Have Fun**

A decade of research has shown us that happiness raises nearly every business outcome. It increases sales by 37%, productivity by 31% and accuracy on tasks by 19%.[49] Yet, it still shocks me how few companies make a point of *ensuring* fun is present in their day-to-day culture. The Norm *says* they want their employees to have fun, but when push comes to shove, happiness is circumvented by the drive for results. It becomes an afterthought. If results are delivered, what remains is a weak and foundationally fragile culture.

Outperformers, too, drive for results but also make it a priority to have fun and celebrate team members for their contributions to your culture (and organization). This is where loyalty is built, and it's a key component to sustained performance excellence.

HIGH PERFORMANCE PEP TALKS

The ability to give an inspiring pep talk that spurs employees, or followers, to better performance is a key skill for any leader. In fact, as a leader, anytime you communicate with someone you're going to either enhance, have no effect or detract from their performance. Language is powerful.

The problem is, when most people hear the term "pep talk," they visualize a Hollywood movie with an ultra-intense coach, barreling into the locker room to scream at a bunch of athletes, in an effort to pump them up.

That's not reality. Or, at least, that's not how things typically operate in the real world. Certainly not in the business world.

Outperformers have a distinct science to their pep talks, as revealed by Harvard Business Review in 2017.[36] They found that motivating, high performance pep talks included three components:

1. Give Direction

Giving direction resides primarily on using "uncertainty-reducing language." (see *Un(certain)ty*) It's the X's and O's, or basic strategy, of *how* to do something. This includes giving simple, clear and understandable instructions, and detail of the performance evaluation.

All of these things actively increase certainty, and the more certain people feel about something, the more likely they are to take decided, intentional action.

2. Demonstrate Empathy

This type of language shows genuine concern for people as human beings. Team members are not just cogs in a wheel that you're trying to turn faster. Empathy can include praise, encouragement, gratitude and acknowledgement of a task's difficulty.

CONNECT TO A PURPOSE

Subtle things like checking on how everyone is doing (as a *person*, not just as a *performer*), appreciating if times are difficult, and letting them know you value their well-being are all demonstrations of empathy.

3. Use Meaning Making Language

Why does this task matter? This links the importance of performing well with the mission and *purpose* behind it (which is why it's included in this chapter).

Typically, meaning making language is best done through stories. These stories should include the difference the work has made for a customer, client, community or the world. It highlights the *real world meaning* behind what you're doing.

On Southwest Airlines' website, you'll find meaningful stories of a military member that traveled home, or a family member that was able to attend a reunion. These connections anchor in the importance of executing on the direction given and fosters a sense of purpose to what you're doing.

Your pep talk recipe should always include these three ingredients, but the amount you use of each is situation specific.

Experienced employees may not need to be given as much direction. A well-established, bonded team may not need as much empathy. If the goals and intention are obvious, it may require less meaning making language.

Still, using these three keys in your next "locker room" pep talk (whether this is live, virtual or email) is the most surefire, scientific way to spur people to better, more purposeful performance.

113

YOU'RE TEACHING, BUT NOT WHAT YOU THINK

"Me and my brother—"

My Mom would politely interrupt. "Scotty, when you're starting a sentence, it's supposed to be, 'My brother and I...'"

Thanks, Mom.

For the bulk of my childhood, my mother was a high school English teacher. It drove me crazy when she'd correct me, but she always said that she only did it to make me better. It took me many years to understand that my Mom's job—teaching English—was not really what she was teaching.

A little over two years ago, she passed away from cancer. When you come from small-town Albany, MN, population 1701, everyone shows up to pay their respects at funerals.

One of the things that struck me about that day were the number of her former students in attendance. Before, and after, the funeral, all of them had a nice thing to say about Mom. She was the type of person that didn't have a mean bone in her body.

One former student walked up to me and said, "Your Mom taught me how to be a good person."

Another one, grinning from ear-to-ear, offered, "She taught me how to stay positive...and to always smile!"

Yet, another student claimed, "She taught me that it's okay to not know the answer; that it's okay to ask for help when you need it."

Of course, in the back of my mind, I'm thinking, "Huh? I thought my Mom's job was to teach *ENGLISH*? Why is no one talking about being taught proper grammar and sentence structure?"

CONNECT TO A PURPOSE

Then it dawned on me—my Mom wasn't teaching these students *English*. She was teaching them valuable, memorable life skills and lessons, disguised as proper grammar and sentence structure.

As a leader, you're doing the same. You might think you're teaching tasks and tactics, software and spreadsheets, projects and procedures, but what you're actually teaching people is something much, much more. Please remember that as you connect to your purpose.

SUMMARY GUIDE

Your purpose is why you exist. Like goals, it should be written down. It's what gets you up in the morning.

What you *say* you do and what you *actually* do are two different things. What you actually do is more meaningful and emotional.

Psychological necessity ties your identity to why you MUST show up and performance with excellence.

Manufacture urgency externally with deadlines, and internally by clarifying the consequences of inaction, selecting the causes of complacency and celebrating small wins.

To have meetings that matter, set crystal clear outcomes, send the agenda in advance, shorten the meeting time, determine if you must be there, minimize participants and end with accountability and responsibility for next steps.

A rallying cry unites and strengthens a team; it makes it distinct.

Great pep talks, online and offline, give direction, demonstrate empathy and use meaning making language.

Remember what you're teaching as a leader. It's purposeful.

SECTION 6

CAST A VISION

"The best is yet to come."

WHERE ARE WE GOING?

Naghmeh Kiumarsi makes fashion that's a statement, not just a style.

In the United States, this pursuit could be seen as ordinary; common. But in Tehran, Iran, it couldn't be more different.

In a country of strict Islamic dress code, where women are expected to be dressed head-to-toe in traditional black hijabs, Naghmeh is a pioneer by introducing color, patterns and textures into the women's wardrobe.

When she rolled out her first designs in 2003, her controversial ideas weren't received well. Why try to fix something so steeped in culture that wasn't necessarily "broken?"

"I believe in the unique style of each person and I want to be able to show another side of Iranian women," she said.

Despite pushback, Naghmeh remained steadfast. She continued to visualize a brighter future for her middle eastern home through fashion. Now, she's attracted a global audience and has received countless messages that she's fundamentally changed the images associated with Iranian women, giving them a unique expression that has never existed.

What's next? "More designs and a broader audience," she says. "The sky is the limit."[37]

A GOOD VISION PAINTS A PICTURE OF THE FUTURE THAT IS NOT YET REALITY.

On a micro, or macro, level, casting a vision shows people where you're going. It gives them a glimpse of a better, brighter future. All

Outperforming leaders do this to inspire action and to give people hope for what is yet to come.

SIMPLE VISIONS SELL

2016 was an unforgettable election in the United States. Regardless of whether you were enamored with the result, we can all agree that it was unlike anything we've ever seen before (and perhaps will ever see again).

There is no greater casting of vision than trying to convince American voters to elect YOU as the next President. You're selling a future dream; where you would like our country to go.

As the process unfolded, researchers analyzed the communication styles of the Republican and Democratic candidates via the *Flesh-Kincaid Test*; a test that assigns a grade-level "readability" score based on the language used in debates and interviews.

Here are the scores they uncovered:[38]

- ✓ Hillary Clinton: 9.18
- ✓ Bernie Sanders: 8.57
- ✓ Ted Cruz: 7.87
- ✓ Marco Rubio: 7.32
- ✓ Jeb Bush: 7.23
- ✓ Donald Trump: 3.96

These results show that a fourth- to fifth-grade level of education is required to understand Trump's language. The average of the other candidates: a ninth-grade level.

In fairness to the other politicians, was Trump elected *because* he communicated in 9- to 11-year-old language? Absolutely not. Elections are decided by a complex interaction of factors that can never be completely understood. But these results underscore one of the most important principles in casting a vision:

SIMPLICITY SELLS.

In other words, do people understand your vision?

Casting a vision is NOT a time to be speaking in complex, technical language. That's not what gives us hope and drives our emotions.

"But, Scott, that's the language my team needs. My industry is complicated!"

I get it, and there's certainly a time and place for that type of language (see strategies in *Communicate Effectively*). **Just not in casting a vision.**

When painting a picture of a future that is not yet reality, keep it simple. If you've been fortunate enough to be a mother or father, could your grade-school or junior-high child understand where you're going?

If they can, you're on the right track.

I'll leave you with five simple visions that anyone, of nearly any age, can understand:

AMAZON: To be earth's most customer centric company.

IKEA: To create a better everyday life for the many people.

NIKE: To bring inspiration and innovation to every athlete* in the world. (*if you have a body, you are an athlete)

TED: We believe passionately in the power of ideas to change attitudes, lives and, ultimately, the world.

TESLA: To accelerate the world's transition to sustainable energy.

USING POSITIVE FUTURE PACING

In 1995, a group of psychologists explored how much impact expectations had on health after a heart transplant. They studied thirty-one patients pre- and post-surgery.

Their findings? Positive expectations of the future led to better mood, adjustment and quality of life, *even in patients who experienced major setbacks*. Higher preoperative expectations also predicted later adherence to a complex medical regimen.[39]

Your expectations of the future can often predict your performance. Better expectations produce better performance.

As a leader it begs the question, how do you create higher expectations for people for the future?

Positive future pacing.

Positive future pacing is a technique often used in NLP (Neuro-Linguistic Programming) by installing positive expectations into your mindset. It allows you to experience the positive results you want to happen *before* they've actually happened.

To simplify, the reason this works is through your brain's association with words. When you hear words like "steak," "sports," or "sell," you make an association of what this word means to you. The positivity or negativity of association will likely define your actions after hearing it.

Future pacing works by using a word that embodies the future, such as:

- ✓ Picture
- ✓ See

- ✓ **Visualize**
- ✓ **Imagine**

To transition this to *positive* future pacing, we simply insert a positive expectation after using the word.

For example, let's say your company is going through an industry downturn and significant internal restructuring. You say to a team member:

***Imagine** how much better you're going to be as a leader after you've gone through these trials and tribulations?*

*Can you **see** how much stronger and more united your department will be now that they've shared this common struggle?*

***Picture** what it will be like once the industry turns up and we are perfectly positioned with our new suite of products?*

Casting a vision is painting a picture that is not yet reality and positive future pacing helps you do it. It may seem subtle—it's only one word, after all—but dripping in this specific language has a profound impact on expectations...and performance.

IMAGES SPEAK LOUDER THAN WORDS

"We are going to run over them like a runaway freight train. We can't, won't be stopped!"

That's the language our coach, Mr. Mader, used before we played in the 1998 State Championship football game. He was casting the vision of how we were going to play that day. And he did it using metaphorical language.

He easily could have said, "We're going to run the ball well," or "We're committed to running the football," but it wouldn't have had near the impact.

A metaphor is a figure of speech that paints a picture in the mind through a comparison. And because our brain processes images between 6 and 600 times faster than words, it helps us to "get it" when we're trying to understand abstract things; especially when the concepts are very complex.[40]

Here are a few simple examples of how metaphors could be used:

- ✓ **Teamwork:** *"Everyone here is a critical piece of the puzzle. Without you, the puzzle is incomplete."*
- ✓ **Proactive vs. Reactive:** *"Be a thermostat, not a thermometer."*
- ✓ **Finish strong:** *"Let's put the icing on the cake."*
- ✓ **Sales:** *"Don't drown people in information."*
- ✓ **Collaboration:** *"The time to build this bridge is now."*
- ✓ **Adversity:** *"We may have been knocked down, but we will always get back up."*
- ✓ **Stay the course:** *"We're on a train ride, not a rollercoaster."*
- ✓ **Change:** *"There's nothing but clear skies up ahead."*

Outperforming leaders are masters at using metaphorical language to create strong images and leave lasting impressions. They get everyone sprinting in the same direction towards a future finish line.

See what I just did there?

*Please take note if you do presentations: more text and numbers on a slide will NOT help people understand something better. You can have numbers on a slide for context, but then use metaphors to help people understand **what the numbers mean**.*

UN(CERTAIN)TY IN FUTURE CHANGE

The future, by definition, is uncertain. Uncertainty, by condition, paralyze people.

Whether it's your family, company, team or direct reports, when we are uncertain, we usually don't act. At the bare minimum, we get a half-hearted, disjointed effort.

CHANGE DOESN'T ALWAYS MEAN YOU'LL MAKE PROGRESS, BUT PROGRESS DOES ALWAYS MEAN MAKING A CHANGE.

The reason we don't take action when we're uncertain is an innate biological response that protects us. Uncertainty causes fear because we *perceive* change in the environment as threatening to our existence as a species.

For The Norm, it's an important distinction. Change almost always means negative, fearful, frightening, worse. Outperformers see it differently.

As a leader, even if the future will always be "uncertain;" your primary objective is to create certainty for people of where you're going. To do this, focus your messaging on two things: giving structure and emphasizing progress.

A sense of structure standardizes a situation. It makes people feel comfortable, safe. Every future situation is unique but applying a what / where / when / how, helps to create structure.

- ✓ **What can be kept the same in the midst of this future change?**

Think tools and technology; the things you use on a daily basis.

- ✓ **Where is the future change happening? Can the location stay the same?**

Think environment; the place where you feel comfortable.

- ✓ **When will daily activities happen?**

Think habits and routines; the timing of your actions.

- ✓ **How will specific tasks be completed?**

Think workflow and collaboration; the way you do things.

If you're going through *any* future change personally or professionally, some of these things will inevitably shift—for the better. The key is to not excessively rock the boat with a dramatic overhaul of everything at once. Reinforce the certain aspects of the what / where / when / how that are remaining consistent. People will feel a greater sense of structure, and thus, take more decided action.

Next, emphasize progress by challenging your people to control the controllables. Focus on how far they've come instead of how far they still have to go (see *Daily Execution. Extraordinary Results.*).

THE BIGGER YOUR VISION FOR FUTURE CHANGE, THE MORE IMPORTANT EMPHASIZING PROGRESS BECOMES.

In 2011, Amabile and Kramer identified the most common event triggering a "best day" for employees was *any* positive progress made by the individual or the team.[41] Progress occurred on a staggering 76% of these days.

It's simple—want your team to have more "best days?" Emphasize their progress. You don't want dark days of doubt and ebbing motivations because they feel the vision is so far away that they'll never get there. Demonstrating ANY progress, no matter how small—during uncertain times verifies that what they're doing is working. It proves that they're going in the right direction; a certain direction.

THE SPECIAL SPEECH STRUCTURE

Nancy Duarte believes that speeches have the power to change the world, and the most effective way of communicating in a speech is through a story.

For her 2013 TEDx talk, she researched some of the best speeches of all time, from Martin Luther King's "I have a dream" speech, Steve Jobs' iPhone launch speech, as well as the Gettysburg Address, and found that they all have a special speech structure.[42]

At the beginning, the speaker describes the status quo, or how things are now. It's painted as dull and underwhelming, and the flaws are highlighted in a specific way that resonates with the audience. Then, they cast the vision of "what could be" in the future, sharply emphasizing the differences between the two. Throughout the middle of the speech, they continue toggling back and forth—with vivid descriptions—between the unappealing status quo and the better, brighter future.

Consider these lines from the *I Have a Dream* speech (notice not only the toggling between status quo and future, but also the metaphors):

CAST A VISION

It is obvious today that America has defaulted on this promissory note insofar as her citizens of color are concerned. Instead of honoring this sacred obligation, America has given the Negro people a bad check, a check which has come back marked "insufficient funds." But we refuse to believe that the bank of justice is bankrupt. We refuse to believe that there are insufficient funds in the great vaults of opportunity of this nation. So we have come to cash this check — a check that will give us upon demand the riches of freedom and the security of justice.[43]

And for Steve Jobs' iPhone launch speech:

The most advanced phones are called smart phones, so they say. And they typically combine a phone plus some e-mail capability, plus they say it's the Internet. It's sort of the baby Internet into one device, and they all have these little plastic keyboards on them. And the problem is that they're not so smart and they're not so easy to use, and so if you kind of make a Business School 101 graph of the smart axis and the easy-to-use axis, phones, regular cell phones are right there, they're not so smart, and they're not so easy to use.

But smartphones are definitely a little smarter, but they actually are harder to use. They're really complicated. Just for the basic stuff people have a hard time figuring out how to use them. Well, we don't want to do either one of these things. What we want to do is make a leapfrog product that is way smarter than any mobile device has ever been and super-easy to use. This is what iPhone is.[44]

Lastly, they end the speech by giving the audience a compelling call to action, encouraging people to adopt the idea and reminding them that, in doing so, it will lead to the better future.

You may look at this and think it doesn't apply to you—but it does. You don't have to be battling for civil rights, launching a revolutionary new product or engaging in a war, to use this special speech structure. When I speak, I'm always comparing and contrasting The Norm (status quo) and Outperform (better future). You can do the same exact thing with where you are now and where you're going.

OUTPERFORM THE NORM

The special "speech" structure is not just for speeches. It's something you can use—online or offline, on a micro or macro level—to cast a leadership vision for the future of your community, team, company or organization. Have one big idea, describe the distinct differences between the ordinary status quo and the extraordinary future, and leave the listeners on a high note with a call to action. You'll be shocked at the results.

SUMMARY GUIDE

A good vision paints a picture of the future that is not yet reality.

Visions can be micro or macro, but are cast the same way.

Simple visions sell. Casting a vision is not a time to use complex, technical language.

Positive future pacing installs positive expectations that allow you to experience results before they're actually happened.
Use words like "picture, see, visualize and imagine."

Your brain processes images faster than words. Using metaphors to create an image helps people understand where you're going.

When we're uncertain, we don't act. Give people structure and emphasize progress to create certainty.

Great speeches continually compare and contrast the status quo and the better, brighter future. They leave people on a high note.

Want to become a stronger visionary leader? See the book bonuses at:
OutperformTheNorm.com/books

SECTION 7

CONSTRUCT YOUR GAME PLAN

"I've never gotten anywhere by standing still."

TOOLS AND PROJECTS

The strategies contained in this book are like tools in your toolbox.

Now that you have the tools, you need to complete your "project." A screwdriver does you no good if the project requires a hammer. And, even if you're reeeeally good with a screwdriver, if the use of a hammer is required, it must be learned. Developed. Solidified. This isn't about identifying your strengths—it's about shoring up your weaknesses to the point that you have none; and all that remains are strengths and greater strengths.

What is the leadership project you'd like to complete? When you identify the project, you can, then, apply and utilize the tools necessary for the job.

I'm using an analogy, but most people say, "I want to be a better leader." It's sort of like embarking on a fitness program and declaring, "I want to get in better shape." There are lots of "shapes"—what does that mean to you? How do *you* define it?

A better leader can mean having a committed mindset, showing up with greater consistency, courageously leading others, communicating more effectively, connecting with a deeper purpose or casting a compelling vision.

All of them are parts of a larger project—being a "better leader"—and, because you're an Outperformer reading this right now, your project is likely already 80-90% complete.

So, what are the underdeveloped, "finishing touches" for your leadership project and what *specific tools* would be required to complete the job?

CONSTRUCT YOUR GAME PLAN

STRATEGIES THAT I CAN USE TO IMPROVE

#1. _____

#2. _____

#3. _____

#4. _____

#5. _____

SITUATIONAL AWARENESS

This car drives itself.

Growing up, this statement would have sounded preposterous. *People* drive cars. Now, it's almost becoming commonplace. When I fly into a city and rent a car, the great majority of current vehicles are semi-autonomous, in which they are able to perform different functions—parallel parking, changing lanes on the highway—with no human assistance.

These cars operate through extreme situational awareness. Their 360-degree ubervision recognizes what is happening in the current moment and anticipates changes in the future surroundings. By scanning the details of the situation and the evolving circumstances, it makes an informed decision.

As leaders, we must operate with similar situational awareness. We're all called upon to lead, personally and professionally, in many different ways. Consider these situational examples:

Personal Leadership Situations
Community, city, neighborhood organizations
Showing up for your family at home
Caring for your elderly parents
Coaching your kid's sports team
Volunteer / non-profit foundations
Church involvement
Hobbies or passion projects

Professional Leadership Situations
Full-team engagements
1-on-1 meetings with direct reports
Meetings with bosses, shareholders, board of directors
Training a new team member
Company-wide events
Appointments with customers or clients
Networking events

The complexities and context of circumstances makes situational awareness key to Outperforming as a leader. It's doubtful that you're going to lead the same way when coaching your kid's sports team as you will when you're meeting with a client. It's also unlikely that you'll show up comparably when training a new team member as you will with your board of directors.

What are your unique leadership situations?

CONSTRUCT YOUR GAME PLAN

MY UNIQUE LEADERSHIP SITUATIONS
Personally OR Professionally

#1. _____

#2. _____

#3. _____

#4. _____

#5. _____

IMPLEMENT WITH INTENTION

If you've made it this far, you're a goal-oriented person. But, for even moderately driven people, goals are almost *never* the limiter. It's the system, method, or process, they use to achieve the goals that determines the difference between The Norm and Outperform.

> **THE NORM WANTS INFORMATION.**
> **OUTPERFORMERS WANT IMPLEMENTATION.**

Specifically, goal achievement is driven by your execution. Preplanning the where, when and how you intend to achieve a goal with an "Implementation Intention" makes it significantly more likely that you'll follow through on a behavior.[45] In this case of *Constructing Your Game Plan*, you're matching a leadership strategy to a specific situation in which it's needed.

The following format is the most advantageous:

> I commit to [PERFORM BEHAVIOR]
> on [DAY, TIME] at [LOCATION]

So, instead of saying, "I'm going to demonstrate more empathy when communicating with my team members," you'd say:

> *I commit to using empathetic language*
> *during my Monday morning team huddle at the office.*

Or, instead of saying, "I will try to listen to more leadership podcasts," you'd say:

> *I commit to managing my inputs by listening to a*
> *new leadership podcast every morning on my commute.*

Implementation intentions combat three of the most common problems in goal achievement: failing to get started, getting derailed, and overextending yourself.[46] Going into each of these individual problems is outside the scope of this book but implementation intentions work because it consciously forces you to think about how you can execute a behavior in your unique situation. It may sound small, but when you map out how you'll implement an intention in advance, it helps you to respond quicker and requires less cognitive resources (*wondering* what you'll do, when), making it more likely that you'll stick with it long-term.

Another benefit of implementation intentions: they depend on the environment, or situation, to drive your behavior—instead of relying on pure motivational horsepower. You don't have to get "motivated" to demonstrate empathy—the Monday morning team huddle sets it in motion. You don't have to get motivated to manage your inputs—the commute to work drives your leadership growth.

CONSTRUCT YOUR GAME PLAN

Outperformers execute the correct game plan to fit a given situation. How can you use the strategies (both the "tools" and the situations) identified in the previous two chapters and rewrite them, so they're implemented with intention?

#1.

I COMMIT TO _____

ON _____ **AT** _____.

#2.

I COMMIT TO _____

ON _____ **AT** _____.

#3.

I COMMIT TO _____

ON _____ **AT** _____.

#4.

I COMMIT TO _____

ON _____ **AT** _____.

#5.

I COMMIT TO _____

ON _____ **AT** _____.

KAIZEN

"I don't know what to write—can you please help me?"

Not long ago, I attended a "fantastic" branding workshop, facilitated by an organization called OrangeBall Creative.

I put *fantastic* in quotes because it was seven hours talking about branding, messaging and marketing for your business. It was a...GRIND (in a good way). My response of not knowing what to write happened multiple times that day; all in response to what I deemed to be painfully simple questions.

But it was "fun" for me to be on the other side of sitting in the audience vs. at the front of the room. I came to appreciate some of the straightforward, tough questions, which require deep, introspective thought, but yield insightful answers.

I can feel this from the audience every time I do a goal achievement workshop. In a nutshell, we only seek to answer five basic questions:

- ✓ Where do you want to go?
- ✓ Why do you want to go there?
- ✓ When will you arrive?
- ✓ How will you get there?
- ✓ What can get in your way?

When I do the presentation, everyone has handouts, and I've found the people that get the most out of it are the ones that think, struggle, grind, and search within themselves for the answers. It is where Outperformers live.

In this workshop, as uncomfortable as it might have been, I was determined to be there, too.

CONSTRUCT YOUR GAME PLAN

I'm not ashamed to admit that I didn't have all the answers. I'm still trying to narrow down my exact target market and to be crystal clear on my messaging. I cannot tell you the number of times that I raised my hand and asked for help, each time fighting off the urge of feeling like an idiot; like everyone else in the room had the answers except me.

It's OK to ask for help, and if you're reading this right now, maybe it resonates with you. Identifying your specific leadership situations or implementing into these with intention may have seemed like a struggle.

That's good!

So often we want to believe that we should have the answers to all the tough questions posed by life—and by business—but that's not the truth. We all need to ask the simple, but tough, questions about how to be the best leader possible to inspire and impact others. When we don't know the answers, we need to check our egos at the door, grind through it, and not be afraid to ask for help.

One of the things they said at the beginning of the workshop is that most people won't take a day out of their schedule to work ON their business. They'll continue to work IN their business.

They're right.

I'd also argue that many people won't take time out of their schedule to work ON their life, goals, ambitions and leadership. I'm convinced one of the reasons we don't do this is because we don't want to be confronted by the fact that we may not know the answers. Better to distract and deflect than to shiver in that cold reality.

Over 30 years ago, Masaaki Imai sat down to write the groundbreaking book, "Kaizen: The Key to Japan's Competitive Success."[50] The term, Kaizen, refers to the Japanese word for "continuous improvement" that was first used by Toyota but is now recognized worldwide as an important pillar in any organization's long-term competitive strategy and quest for superior results. It combines personal discipline, with teamwork, small steps, and suggestions for improvement. The end result is a change for better (*Kai* = change; *Zen* = for the better).

**TO CHANGE FOR THE BETTER:
IT IS WHY WE ARE HERE ON THIS PLANET.**

Going forward, take the time to ask tough questions—about your leadership; about your life. Continue improving *you*, because you cannot get the best out of others if you're unable to get the best out of yourself. Then, continue improving *others*, because the world needs more committed, consistent and courageous leaders. Those that influence and inspire people to see more, do more and become more, in the pursuit of a lofty goal or worthwhile ambition.

It has been a privilege serving you.

Keep Outperforming,

ACKNOWLEDGMENTS

Almost every "Acknowledgments" section that I read in books, aims to thank specific individuals for helping them along the way. I'm going to partially go against the grain and not do that.

Sure, I've had *plenty* of people who have contributed to these pages, but I'm blessed and fortunate to be able to speak to small and large groups for a living. Even though I'm technically brought in as a "teacher;" I've found myself being more of a "student." It has been a distinct honor and privilege to converse with so many people, in so many industries, over the last few years. I've learned more lessons about real-world leadership through these interactions than I ever could have otherwise.

Therefore, I'll acknowledge mostly organizations—and a few individuals—that are responsible for bringing this book to fruition.

I'm always asked how I got started as a speaker. The answer: Rotary Clubs. No one knew who the heck I was and I desperately wanted to get my message out into the world. They let me do that, all 44 of them around Minneapolis-St. Paul and Denver. Thank you, Rotarians. I love your charity and mission.

PMI (Project Management Institute) Chapters, particularly Minnesota (Janice Pyka), Northeast WI, Milwaukee, Chicagoland, Central Illinois (Malati Penumudy) Mid-Missouri, Mile Hi (Jim Escue) and Pikes Peak. This is one of my favorite organizations for which to speak.

Particular random companies and organizations that have impacted me: Cretex Companies, Northwestern Mutual, Edward Jones, Borgert Products (thanks, Sue!), Dalseth Dental (Pascal, let's ride!), DJO Global, State Farm, Sherwin Williams, Sales & Marketing Executives, Professional Sales Association, Legacy Building Solutions, Minneapolis Oxygen Company, Tennessee Association for Home Care and Navigate Forward.

Two other people who deserve shout outs:

OUTPERFORM THE NORM

Bob Willbanks of Ambassadors for Business (AFB) and Thrive Events: You're one of the best guys I know and I'm beyond impressed with the work you're doing.

Don Salverda, I cannot begin to tell you how awed I am with your commitment to growth and development. When I say, "leaders are readers," there's no better example than you. You were also one of the first people who believed in me as a speaker—you might not even remember it, but you long ago told me I was "good." I'll never forget that.

Lastly, I received a rare piece of negative feedback from a speaking engagement a little over a year ago. It came via an anonymous survey after the event had concluded.

"Scott needs to wait about 20 years, then maybe he'll figure out leadership."

I was warned by the organizers ahead of time that there's one person who always leaves these comments. Still, it stung.

I'm sorry, anonymous sir, I didn't wait 20 years. I waited one. I don't have it "figured out" and I probably never will. Nor will you. Nor will any of us. But your comment motivated me, and made me buckle down to read the latest research and write my best book possible. Thank you for the inspiration ☺

REFERENCES

1. *What is leadership?* Retrieved from https://www.forbes.com/sites/kevinkruse/2013/04/09/what-is-leadership/#5347d1a5b90c

2. *7 Scientifically Proven Benefits of Gratitude.* Retrieved from https://www.psychologytoday.com/us/blog/what-mentally-strong-people-dont-do/201504/7-scientifically-proven-benefits-gratitude

3. *Mastery Orientation.* Retrieved from https://link.springer.com/referenceworkentry/10.1007%2F978-0-387-79061-9_1722

4. *Stanford psychologist: Achievement goals can be shaped by environment.* Retrieved from https://news.stanford.edu/news/2012/may/shape-achievement-goals-051012.html

5. *Our Brain's Negativity Bias.* Retrieved from https://www.psychologytoday.com/us/articles/200306/our-brains-negative-bias

6. *Mental and Emotional Benefits of Activity.* Retrieved from https://www.healthlinkbc.ca/physical-activity/mental-and-emotional-benefits

7. *The Hydration Equation: Update on Water Balance and Cognitive Performance.* Retrieved from https://www.ncbi.nlm.nih.gov/pmc/articles/PMC4207053/

8. *Plan Ahead and Increase Productivity.* Brian Tracy, Retrieved from https://www.briantracy.com/blog/time-management/plan-ahead-and-increase-productivity/

9. *What are Attributional and Explanatory Styles in Psychology?* Retrieved from https://positivepsychology.com/explanatory-styles-optimism/

10. *Overcoming Imposter Syndrome.* Retrieved from https://hbr.org/2008/05/overcoming-imposter-syndrome

11. *It's Not Just You: These Super Successful People Suffer From Imposter Syndrome.* Retrieved from https://www.fastcompany.com/40447089/its-not-just-you-these-super-successful-people-suffer-from-imposter-syndrome

12. *Rising Star Coach P.J. Fleck Proving He's More Than Antics with 8-0 Minnesota.* Retrieved from https://bleacherreport.com/articles/2861757-rising-star-coach-pj-fleck-proving-hes-more-than-antics-with-8-0-minnesota

13. *Why It's Hard to Admit to Being Wrong.* Retrieved from https://www.npr.org/templates/story/story.php?storyId=12125926?storyId=12125926

14. *Becoming Cary Grant.* The Atlantic, Retrieved from https://www.theatlantic.com/magazine/archive/2007/01/becoming-cary-grant/305548/

15. *How Ford did it.* Retrieved from https://archive.fortune.com/2011/01/12/autos/Bill-Ford-Alan-Mulally-carmaker.fortune/index.htm

16. *Maslow's Hierarchy of Needs.* Retrieved from https://www.simplypsychology.org/maslow.html

17. *Top 10 Fears That Hold People Back in Life.* Retrieved from https://www.psychologytoday.com/us/blog/what-mentally-strong-people-dont-do/202001/top-10-fears-hold-people-back-in-life

18. *PR Nightmares: United Fiasco Among Worst Corporate Gaffes.* Retrieved from https://www.bloomberg.com/news/articles/2017-04-12/pr-nightmares-united-seat-fiasco-among-worst-corporate-gaffes

19. *Read United CEO's 3 statements on passenger dragged off flight.* Retrieved from https://www.boston.com/travel/business/2017/04/11/read-united-ceos-3-statements-on-passenger-dragged-off-flight

20. *Top stats to know: Bo Ryan's best numbers.* Retrieved from https://www.espn.com/blog/statsinfo/post/_/id/112573/top-stats-to-know-bo-ryans-best-numbers

21. *Intuition and unconscious thought.* Retrieved from https://www.researchgate.net/publication/289541850_Intuition_and_unconscious_thought

22. *Examining Differential Coaching Behaviors in Positive Coaches: A Mixed-Method Perspective Guided by the Expectation-Performance Process.* Retrieved from https://www.researchgate.net/publication/330563012_Examining_Differential_Coaching_Behaviors_in_Positive_Coaches_A_Mixed-Methods_Perspective_Guided_by_the_Expectation_Performance_Process

23. *You Want It When? Retrieved from* https://www.i4cp.com/news/2007/06/26/you-want-it-when

24. *Why Aren't You Delegating?* Retrieved from https://www.i4cp.com/news/2007/06/26/you-want-it-when

25. *Google's Project Aristotle re: Work. Guide: Understanding team effectiveness.* Retrieved from https://rework.withgoogle.com/print/guides/5721312655835136/

26. *An Overview of the Influence of the Physical Office Towards Employees.* Retrieved from https://www.sciencedirect.com/science/article/pii/S1877705811029730

27. *Podiatry: Foot Facts.* Retrieved from http://www.bridgewater.nhs.uk/wp-content/uploads/2012/11/Foot-Facts.pdf

28. *What is Your Purpose in Life? (Actual Examples and Answers).* Retrieved from https://www.trackinghappiness.com/life-purpose-examples/

29. *High Performance Habits: How Extraordinary People Become That Way.* Brendon Burchard, Hay House, Inc.

30. *What is Loss Aversion?* Retrieved from https://www.psychologytoday.com/us/blog/science-choice/201803/what-is-loss-aversion

31. *Ringelmann Effect.* Retrieved from http://psychology.iresearchnet.com/social-psychology/group/ringelmann-effect/

32. *Why Less is More in Teams.* Harvard Business Review, Retrieved from https://hbr.org/2012/08/why-less-is-more-in-teams

REFERENCES

33. *The Science and Fiction of Meetings.* Retrieved from https://www.researchgate.net/publication/265508855_The_Science_and_Fiction_of_Meetings

34. *This Weekly Meeting Took Up 300,000 Hours a Year.* Retrieved from https://hbr.org/2014/04/how-a-weekly-meeting-took-up-300000-hours-a-year

35. *Jeff Bezos's Productivity Tip? The '2 Pizza Rule'* Retrieved from https://www.inc.com/business-insider/jeff-bezos-productivity-tip-two-pizza-rule.html

36. *The Science of Pep Talks.* Harvard Business Review, Retrieved from https://hbr.org/2017/07/the-science-of-pep-talks

37. *The CNN 10 Visionary Women.* Retrieved from https://www.cnn.com/interactive/2014/03/living/cnn10-visionary-women/

38. *The Readability and Simplicity of Donald Trump's Language:* Retrieved from https://www.researchgate.net/publication/319697409_The_Readability_and_Simplicity_of_Donald_Trump's_Language

39. *Positive expectations predict health after heart transplantation.* Retrieved from https://psycnet.apa.org/record/1995-18688-001?doi=1

40. *Research: Is A Picture Worth 1,000 Words Or 60,000 Words in Marketing*? Retrieved from https://www.emailaudience.com/research-picture-worth-1000-words-marketing/

41. *The Power of Small Wins.* Retrieved from https://hbr.org/2011/05/the-power-of-small-wins

42. *The secret structure of great talks.* Nancy Duarte, Retrieved from https://www.ted.com/talks/nancy_duarte_the_secret_structure_of_great_talks#t-372753

43. *I have a dream.* Martin Luther King, Jr. Retrieved from https://www.archives.gov/files/press/exhibits/dream-speech.pdf

44. *Steve Jobs iPhone 2007 Presentation (full transcript).* Retrieved from https://singjupost.com/steve-jobs-iphone-2007-presentation-full-transcript/

45. *Implementation Intentions Facilitate Action Control.* Retrieved from https://www.psychologytoday.com/us/blog/dont-delay/201001/implementation-intentions-facilitate-action-control

46. *Implementation Intentions.* Retrieved from http://psychology.iresearchnet.com/social-psychology/control/implementation-intentions/

47. *Why Culture Eats Strategy for Breakfast.* Retrieved from http://crmsearch.eu/culture-eats-strategy.php

48. *What We Live By.* Retrieved from https://www.zappos.com/about/what-we-live-by

49. *The Happiness Dividend.* Retrieved from https://hbr.org/2011/06/the-happiness-dividend

50. *What is Kaizen.* Retrieved from https://www.kaizen.com/what-is-kaizen.html

ABOUT THE AUTHOR

SCOTT WELLE is a #1 international best-selling author, speaker and founder of Outperform The Norm, a global movement that coaches athletes and business leaders to raise their game and perform at the highest level.

While the rest of the competition is playing not to lose, Scott teaches people to play to win. His proprietary "Commit / Attack / Conquer" formula ensures people fall asleep at night knowing they are making the most of their precious days on this planet. For this, Fox 9 in Minneapolis-St Paul has called him a *"Motivational Expert."*

Scott has always loved sports but felt he underperformed early in his career by not mastering the "mental game." After graduating with his Master's degree in Sport Psychology, he made it his life's mission to coach people to higher levels of performance and not let others repeat his mistakes. Throughout this process, he's realized how the same mental principles that allow athletes to be successful will allow business leaders to achieve exceptional results, and this formed the foundation for Outperform The Norm.

Now, Scott's best-selling books, articles, videos and podcasts inspire hundreds of thousands of people worldwide and students in over 35 countries have taken his online courses. He is an adjunct professor at St. Olaf University and serves on advisory committees of three national level organizations. He regularly coaches top performing executives, sales professionals and entrepreneurs, as well as elite athletes, all with one common goal: to OUTPERFORM.

Scott enjoys pushing his own physical and mental limits, completing five Ironman triathlons, 29 marathons, R2R2R (47 miles back and forth

ABOUT THE AUTHOR

through the Grand Canyon) and a 100-mile ultra marathon run. He is very close with his brother, Jason. Together they "plod" at least one marathon together each year, laughing the whole way.

Please visit him at ScottWelle.com.

ALSO BY SCOTT WELLE

OUTPERFORM THE NORM

Health. Happiness. High Performance.

OutperformTheNorm.com/books

OUTPERFORM THE NORM
for Sales

The 50 Best Tips EVER for Successful Selling

OutperformTheNorm.com/books

OUTPERFORM THE NORM
for Student Athletes

Perform Your Best in Sports, School and LIFE

OutperformTheNorm.com/books